East European International Road Haulage

Originally published in 1992, this study examines and analyses the role, planning and operation of international road hauliers based in the former East European countries. It outlines the problems they faced and the opportunities the new model of Europe should have provided at the time. It also emphasizes the role that West European hauliers could play in the market and the activities that the European Community carried out in this field in the light of 1992. It concludes by stressing the actions needed in the near future by governments and operators alike. Today it can be read in its historical context.

East European International Road Haulage

Michael Roe

Routledge
Taylor & Francis Group

First published in 1992
by Avebury (Ashgate Publishing Limited)

This edition first published in 2022 by Routledge
2 Park Square, Milton Park, Abingdon, Oxon, OX14 4RN

and by Routledge
605 Third Avenue, New York, NY 10017

Routledge is an imprint of the Taylor & Francis Group, an informa business

© 1992 M. Roe

Publisher's Note
The publisher has gone to great lengths to ensure the quality of this reprint but points out that some imperfections in the original copies may be apparent.

Disclaimer
The publisher has made every effort to trace copyright holders and welcomes correspondence from those they have been unable to contact.

A Library of Congress record exists under LCCN: 92027951

ISBN: 978-1-032-18551-4 (hbk)
ISBN: 978-1-003-25510-9 (ebk)
ISBN: 978-1-032-18556-9 (pbk)

Book DOI 10.4324/9781003255109

East European International Road Haulage

MICHAEL ROE
University of Plymouth

Avebury

Aldershot · Brookfield USA · Hong Kong · Singapore · Sydney

Published by

Avebury
Ashgate Publishing Limited
Gower House
Croft Road
Aldershot
Hants GU11 3UR
England

Ashgate Publishing Company
Old Post Road
Brookfield
Vermont 05036
USA

A CIP catalogue record for this book is available from the British Library and the US Library of Congress.

ISBN 1 85628 310 0

Printed and Bound in Great Britain by
Athenaeum Press Ltd., Newcastle upon Tyne.

Contents

Acknowledgements   vi

1   Introduction   1

2   International Trucking in Europe   7

3   CMEA Trade with the European Community   22

4   The Eastern Bloc Road Haulage Markets   49

5   Bulgaria   68

6   Czechoslovakia   85

7   Hungary   102

8   Poland   130

9   Conclusions   147

10 References   165

Acknowledgements

Thanks to Lyn Stott and Sue Blackman for all the patient word processing. To Liz, Joseph and Sian for the weeks away from home, and to the staff of the Hotel Polom, Zilina, Czechoslovakia for finding a television on the night England played West Germany in the semi-final of the World Cup.

With thanks also to the Economic and Social Committee of the European Communities and the National Westminster Bank for permission to quote extensively from their publications. Permission is being sought from the Commission for the European Committee for further quotations.

1 Introduction

This study emerged from a widespread recognition in Western European commercial circles that East European countries were operating unfair practices in the administration, financing and operation of transport services in general and international road haulage in particular. This was a particular concern for CMEA (Council for Mutual Economic Assistance) - EC (European Community) traffic and specifically, the effect on EC road haulage operators.

For the purposes of this research, Eastern Europe has been confined to the European members of the CMEA, excluding the Soviet Union. Consequently it includes Bulgaria, Czechoslovakia, DDR, Hungary, Poland and Romania, but excludes Albania and Yugoslavia. The choice of these six members was made for a number of reasons:

(i)   It includes the major participants in the EC-CMEA international road haulage market. The Soviet Union although operating a large number of international trucks, concentrates rather more on USSR-Scandinavian, and USSR-East European trade.

(ii)   They have until recently all pursued very similar economic programmes in line, largely, with CMEA policies.

(iii)   Constraints in terms of time and resources precluded a larger study, thus contributing to the need to exclude the Soviet Union.

(iv)   Data was more freely available from these six, albeit still heavily constrained.

Funding for the research has come from the Commission of the European Communities covering a period of one year from September 1989 to October 1990. Consequently this study covers policy and operations within the six chosen states during that period and immediately preceding it.

The research had a number of detailed objectives which have directed progress:

(i)   In the absence of widely available data on road haulage to and from the CMEA countries, a prime objective was to gather together as much information as possible on the structure of the road haulage industry, the commodities carried, their origins and destinations, the operating characteristics of the Eastern Bloc fleets including vehicle types and quality, pricing and costs, and the economic and financial regime under which they must operate. Clearly this was likely to be a difficult task given the widely recognised problems of extracting meaningful and accurate commercial information from the East. At the commencement of the project, almost no reliable data was freely available for any of the six countries concerned, on international road haulage, policy and operation.

(ii)   To establish the balance of trade carried between EC and CMEA hauliers in the international market. There is a widely held belief that the Eastern Bloc takes a disproportionate share of international traffic between east and west Europe, and vice versa (for example see ESCEC, 1977) but evidence to support this assumption, particularly up to date information, was scarce.

(iii)   Given that an imbalance in traffic might exist, there was a major aim to establish whether unfair commercial practices existed in the Eastern Bloc, enabling them to compete and gain traffic that they rightly should not carry, thus imposing unfair commercial pressure upon competing West European hauliers. Consequently, issues of backhaul availability, subsidy, insurance and visa constraints, fuel availability, unfair trading practices and other related issues needed to be investigated.

(iv)   The impact of the Single European Act and the consequential harmonisation and liberalisation of the road haulage industry in Western Europe, and its effect upon the international trucking industry outside the EC were also important objectives. How far would liberalisation enable a more efficient and streamlined Western European fleet to compete internationally with the CMEA fleets? What were the views and fears of the Eastern Bloc in terms of a more efficient West European road haulage industry? How were the CMEA fleets preparing for the advent of the Single European Market?

(v)   Given the notable increase in trade between East and West Europe during the late 1980's and the development of 'perestroika' with its prospects of increasing trade, how could West and East European international road transport co-operate to make the transport of freight more efficient, effective and competitive? Whilst the research was being conducted, these issues became more and more significant.

(vi)   Finally, what should be the actions and policies of the EC to stimulate international trade and transport in this market and how could western hauliers be made more competitive in the light of the unfair commercial practices of the Eastern Bloc - if they existed?

The research was conducted during a period of remarkable change in Eastern Europe - political, social and economic - changes which have had profound impacts on every aspect of commercial life including that of international road haulage. To note just a few of the changes that have occurred during this period:

3

(i)	Poland	- beginning of non-Communist Government
		- creation of a free market
		- convertibility of currency
		- privatisation of State haulage
		- growth of unemployment
		- massive price rises
		- hugely fluctuating inflation
		- IMF and other international loans
		- partial subsidy removal

(ii)	Hungary	- free elections
		- removal of the Communist Party from State organisations
		- encouragement of free enterprise
		- growth of unemployment
		- partial subsidy removal
		- IMF and other international loans

(iii)	Czechoslovakia	- free elections
		- dismantling of Communist Party infrastructure
		- partial subsidy removal
		- encouragement of free enterprise

(iv)	DDR	- free elections
		- dismantling of Communist Party infrastructure
		- currency union with West Germany
		- moves towards German unification
		- privatisation of road haulage
		- introduction of joint ventures

| (v) | Romania | - free elections |
| | | - economic, political and social chaos |

(vi)	Bulgaria	- free elections
		- Communists retain power
		- some relaxation of State economic control

Inevitably these changes, plus the many others not outlined above, have had implications for the research programme and the results of the studies carried out. Discussions with the Romanian State authorities before Christmas 1989, for example, remained extremely interesting but needed complete revision by January 1990 to ensure a full picture of constantly changing developments. Certainly the international road haulage industry is now operating in a very difficult and different environment from that at the commencement of the research. Consequently, further work is needed in Eastern Europe, to monitor the commercial impacts.

The result of all these changes is that another objective of the research could be added to those noted above:

-       to establish how the EC could aid the process of economic reform in the CMEA countries, with specific reference to the international haulage sector.

Any research into road haulage, its operation and economics, faces difficulties in obtaining reliable, comprehensive and meaningful data. Quite understandably, in the West, hauliers are frequently reluctant to reveal commercial policies and agreements and are unwilling to discuss prices, conditions and contracts in any detail. This is also true of the East. However, in Eastern Europe there are also two other problems which will take some time to be resolved:

(i)   the general inadequacy in management information that exists in East European commerce. International road haulage is no exception to this problem. There is little monitoring of operations or policies, little data available, and a lack of management information systems to process this data if any exists;

(ii)   the bureaucratic structures of East Europe which make contacting relevant industries difficult, let alone extracting relevant information from them once they are contacted.

Both problems have made the extraction of information from Eastern European hauliers a problematic task, but through a combination of previous established contacts, perseverance, and luck, sufficient information from Poland, Hungary, Czechoslovakia and Bulgaria in particular, has been obtained, to provide a detailed picture of East European operational practice and future problems and policies.

The remainder of this text is divided into a number of sections dealing with the structure of the international road haulage market in Europe, the East/West trade situation, discussion of previous work in this area, and an analysis of the markets in each of the CMEA countries. It concludes with an examination of the effects of the completion of the Single European Market on CMEA/EC transport, the effect of changes taking place in Eastern Europe, and the need for further research to establish how the European Community can help to encourage further economic change and developments.

2 International trucking in Europe

Introduction

The United Nations Convention of 1949 gave limited rights to vehicle operators in signatory countries, to take their vehicles on the territory of other signatory countries. These rights, however, did not relieve the operators of their need to tax their vehicles in each country that they wished to visit, obtain the necessary licences to operate and to meet fully, all of the requirements of traffic legislation in each country.

Prior to the 1960's these constraints were unimportant to many countries in Europe since international road haulage remained a relatively minor mode of transport. However, with the improvements in roads and vehicles, the advent of the roll on/roll off ferry, changes in marketing, and changes in commodity characteristics, requiring a more controlled and efficient distribution service than could be offered by rail, sea or canal alone, the international road haulage industry began to expand, and consequently the need for an improved system of agreements became urgent. The result was the system of bilateral agreements which now exists covering the vast majority of pairs of countries of both East and West Europe, dictating the provision of permits allowing the provision of international road haulage services. Their prime aim is to facilitate

7

hauliers' movements throughout Europe, avoiding the need for each operator to apply to each foreign state's government for each trip. It is only in recent years, and within the European Community alone, that the bilateral permit regime is being dismantled with the objective of liberalising the market. Elsewhere in Europe it remains dominant.

Bilateral Agreements

Table 1 gives an indication of the bilateral agreements that exist between the twelve members of the European community and the six of the CMEA with which this research report is concerned.

Coverage is only partial. Notable are the missing arrangements between Portugal and Hungary, DDR, and Poland; Luxembourg with Hungary and Romania; West Germany with Hungary and Czechoslovakia; Spain with the DDR; and Eire with all CMEA countries.

These gaps in agreements are, however, largely explicable. Portugal has a relatively small trucking industry, and lies far from East Europe, thus the maritime mode is dominant for transport. Spain is in a similar position although its trucking industry is far bigger. Eire is a maritime nation, far removed from East Europe and with few trade links. Luxembourg is a small nation with only relatively small trucking interests. The main inexplicable failure to make agreements centres on West Germany and Hungary/Czechoslovakia.

The majority of road traffic between the EC and the CMEA countries is carried under bilateral agreements. Where these do not exist, special agreement has to be reached between the two countries concerned.

Agreements are administered by joint committees consisting of officials from the Governmental transport ministries of the two respective countries. Each joint committee meets on an 'ad hoc' basis although in many cases these are regular and annual, particularly between countries with a significant trade pattern. The maximum time period without a meeting is normally designated as five years. More frequent meetings commonly take place between countries which enforce restrictive quota and permit restrictions.

TABLE 1

BILATERAL AGREEMENTS BETWEEN THE EC AND EASTERN EUROPE AT 1.4.1990

	BUL	H	ROM	DDR	POL	CZ
UK	72	70	69	74	75	70
LUX	89	82	89	82		
E	78	80	79	78	79	
PORT	79	78				
F	60	66	66	75	68	68
D	80	70	72	69		
NL	70	70	68	74	70	67
B	69	67	84	73	68	68
GCE	64	77	74	81	77	77
I	68	68	66	77	68	66
DK	68	75	67	73	72	69
IRL						*

* Advanced state of preparation

Bilateral agreements normally cover the following issues:

(i)   The types of transport operations which are permitted to or through the territories of the partner countries. Thus a journey, say from France to Romania by a French haulier would be subject to the bilateral agreements that exist between France and Romania, West Germany, Austria and Hungary (dependent on the route chosen). This often has ramifications for route choice in that countries improving severe permit restrictions may be avoided. The result is that the 'lowest common denominator' effect applies, in that, for example, the lowest maximum weight limit allowed 'en route' has to be adhered to.

(ii)   The prohibition of national transport operations on the territory of one country by operators from the other country (ie. cabotage).

(iii)   Requirements, if any, relating to permits.

(iv)   Rules regarding third country traffic. (The carriage of a load from or to the partner country coming from or going to a country other than the operator's home country).

(v)   Procedures for reviewing the agreement. (Normally by setting up a joint committee).

(vi)   Procedures for dealing with infringements of the provisions of the agreement by operators from either country.

(vii)   Some agreements include provisions relating to the regulation of passenger transport and mutual exemption from vehicle taxation.

Bilateral agreements fall broadly into three types:

(i)   those not requiring permits and not subject to a quota limiting the number of goods vehicle movements;

(ii)   those requiring permits but not imposing a quota, or ones that impose a quota so large that there is effectively no quantitative restriction on operations;

(iii)   those requiring permits and applying restrictive quotas such that there are insufficient permits to meet demand.

Restrictive numbers of quotas are imposed for a number of reasons:

(i)   Because the country concerned may wish to encourage traffic to move by rail or inland waterway. This is a frequent reason in Eastern Europe.

(ii)   Because they may wish to protect their own indigenous haulage industry.

(iii)   To protect their own road infrastructure.

Almost without exception, the more restrictive bilateral agreements are at the request of the East European partners who use them as a way of restraining the activities of a more efficient and highly competitive West European haulage industry, as a means of directing traffic by mode, and as a bureaucratic hurdle.

The agreements relating to EC-CMEA traffic contains main types of permit for international road haulage:

(i)   General Quota Permits - the most commonly used permit. Operators need a general quota permit to cover each return journey either to or through the country requiring the permit. For some countries, these permits can be converted into multiple journey or period permits with some cost savings.

(ii)   Non-Quota Permits - some traffic requires permits but is not subject to the general quota (for example, all traffic to or through Czechoslovakia from the UK is subject to non quota permits). Generally speaking, such permits are restrictive in terms of the types of operation that can be carried out.

Other Conventions

Apart from the system of bilateral agreements, quotas and permits, there are a number of other conventions and regimes under which international road haulage operates between the European Community and the countries of the CMEA.

(i) CMR Convention

CMR is a United Nations Convention defining the rights and obligations of the sender and the carrier in any contract for the international carriage of goods by road. It applies only to contracts for the carriage of goods by road for hire and reward where the journey takes place on the territory of at least two different countries, at least one of which is a contracting party to the convention.

Within the European community all countries are contracting parties with the exception of the Republic of Ireland. All CMEA countries are signed members. Hence all international road journeys for hire and reward are subject to the convention.

(ii) Dangerous Goods

The main agreement concerning the International Carriage of Dangerous Goods by Road is the ADR, entering force from 1968. It controls packing and labelling of dangerous goods and prescribes technical requirements for the vehicles carrying them.

Within the European Community, all twelve countries are party to the agreement with the exception of the Republic of Ireland and Greece. In the CMEA countries, only Bulgaria and Romania are not party to the agreement. Thus, only a very limited number of international journeys between the EC and the CMEA countries are not subject to ADR controls.

(iii) Perishable Foodstuffs

Transportation of perishable foodstuffs by international road services is conducted under the ATP agreement negotiated by the United Nations. The aim is to facilitate the international carriage of such foodstuffs, to raise standards, to promote competition and to protect public health. It thus lays down technical standards and procedures for equipment, including vehicles.

Romania and Hungary are the CMEA members not party to the agreement. Portugal and Greece are similarly EC members not parties. Thus, most international road movements between the EC and the CMEA countries are covered by the ATP agreement.

(iv) Drivers' Hours

International road transport between the European Community and the CMEA countries is subject to the AETR rules on drivers' hours in Czechoslovakia and the DDR. When driving within the Community, operators from both groups are subject to the EC regulations. When driving in areas of the CMEA other than Czechoslovakia and the DDR, national rules apply. In practice drivers who keep to the EC rules are unlikely to encounter any difficulties within the CMEA area.

(v) TIR

TIR is an international convention introduced by the United Nations. The original convention was introduced in 1959 and has now largely been replaced by that of 1975. The underlying purpose of the system is to allow goods carrying vehicles to be sealed at their point of departure and to travel, generally unhindered other than for checks on seals and documentation, to the point of destination. All EC and CMEA countries are contracting parties to the convention. Consequently, the vast majority of movements between the EC and CMEA countries are conducted under TIR regulations, when suitable vehicles are used.

(vi) Insurance

All international haulage has to take place against the background of national laws on transport insurance. Throughout the EC and CMEA, insurance against third party risks is compulsory. The Green Card scheme applies to all the EC, but only Czechoslovakia and the DDR are CMEA members. Romania, Hungary and Poland are not members of the Green Card scheme, but do require third party insurance.

Consequently, all countries in the EC and CMEA operating internationally are subject to the same basic insurance regulations. However, as we shall see later, there are marked differences between the groups, particularly in terms of costs.

(vii) Other Documentation

There are a variety of documentary regulations relating to international road goods movements that also apply - including those relating to driver's licences, passports, vehicle excise licences, operators licences and regulation documents. Many of them are uncontentious and any relevant issues will be raised in the next section dealing with the individual CMEA countries.

The CMEA Countries

Given the basic issues discussed above, we can now turn to the six CMEA countries and analyse the detailed requirements each places upon EC operators entering their national space. In later chapters we shall examine the operators from the same CMEA countries to establish their operating policies, practices and economics in comparison with the conditions placed upon the EC hauliers in the international road freight market.

(i) Bulgaria

European Community operators, generally speaking, may carry goods to, through or from Bulgaria and also enter Bulgaria with an empty vehicle to collect a return load. Also, generally speaking, an operator from the European Community may carry goods between Bulgaria and a third country and vice versa, provided this is permitted by the terms of the bilateral agreements concluded between the three countries concerned. Hence, theoretically, Bulgaria operates a fairly liberal regime concerning international road haulage relations. Practical considerations will be covered in a later chapter.

No permits are needed for European Community vehicles to operate to or through Bulgaria.

Various requirements are placed upon the EC haulier:

- a Green Card insurance certificate should be carried, even though Bulgaria is not a members of the scheme;
- the vehicle registration document is needed;
- TIR carnets are accepted;
- a full passport, visa and EC driving licence is necessary;
- Bulgarian national driving laws must be respected, but they tend to be more liberal than those of the EC;
- no transit taxes are charged;
- a full tank of fuel may be imported.

Operationally, there are a number of important constraints to note.

Only twenty designated filling stations exist where fuel for international lorries is available. Purchase of fuel is only available using 'Skipka' coupons, purchased for convertible currency at the border. In addition, there are twenty other filling stations where credit cards (in convertible currency) can be used.

Vehicle spares for Western built lorries are available, but only through the State owned 'Bulgarianteravto-service', and for convertible currency. In addition, almost any service, facility or technical assistance is available with convertible currency, and almost none without it.

(ii) Czechoslovakia

European Community operators may carry loads to, from and through Czechoslovakia and may enter the country with an empty vehicle to collect a return load. Operators from the EC may only engage in traffic between Czechoslovakia and a third country or vice versa if they are in possession of an extra 'special' permit authorising them to do so, and issued by their own international road freight office. There are no bilateral agreements between West Germany or the Republic of Ireland and Czechoslovakia, although the latter is in an advanced state of preparation. Cabotage is prohibited for EC operators. Hence, overall, Czechoslovakia is only slightly less liberal than Bulgaria in its theoretical attitude to EC hauliers.

Own account EC operators require permits to enter Czechoslovakia but these are not subject to quota arrangements. Hire and reward operators can obtain permits easily, if from Western Europe, but less easily if from the East - possibly reflecting the desire for hard currency from the former. Certain specialised transport is exempt from permit requirements.

Other requirements or regulations include:

- the need to carry a Green Card document;
- the need to carry the vehicle registration document;
- TIR carnets are accepted;
- full passports, visas and driving licences are necessary;
- Czechoslovakian national driving laws apply, but are generally more liberal than the EC;
- no transit taxes are applied;
- a full tank of fuel may be imported.

Western vehicle spares are not readily available from any source, and hard currency is needed to obtain them, if at all. Breakdown facilities are also only available for hard currency.

(iii) DDR

Economic and political changes affecting the DDR from 1990 have markedly affected the operation and management of road haulage. The following section attempts to describe the position at the time of the changes.

European Community operators can carry goods to, from and through the DDR and may enter the country with an empty vehicle to collect a return load. This country traffic and cabotage are shortly prohibited.

However, it is generally recognised and even formally noted in advice to international road hauliers in the West, that all DDR imports and exports are either transported by rail or ship, or are carried by vehicles owned by the previously State owned international haulier, VEB Deutrans.

In theory, no permits are required by European Community hauliers in the fairly rare event (until 1990) of carrying goods to and from the DDR. However, in practice, the appropriate documentation for imports has to be supplied by the DDR State Foreign Trade Enterprise customer, and carried by the haulier. To carry exports, an 'abfordeningschein' had to be acquired from VEB Deutrans themselves, at least four days in advance. The system was slow, administratively complex and designed to inhibit the use of Western European hauliers.

Since the process towards German unification has commenced, these constraints now largely do not apply, but up until early 1990 they represented possibly the most severely restrictive regime for international haulage in the Eastern Bloc.

Commonly, European Community vehicles still need to cross the DDR to gain access to Poland and occasionally the USSR. Here, a 'transitwarenbegleitschein' is needed and must be acquired five days in advance from VEB Deutrans.

No vehicle or transit taxes are payable.

Western vehicle spares were largely unobtainable and any purchase of spares or most other items, needed to be in convertible currency. All this has now altered. Green Cards remain a necessity, as is the vehicle registration document, passport and international driving licence. Visas were required until July 1990. TIR carnets are accepted.

The political and economic changes in the DDR have made most of the constraints relating to international haulage in the past, now redundant - or are soon to be. For this reason and that of associated events such as true currency convertibility, the DDR was exempted from the remainder of the study. However, its restrictive regime up until 1990 should be noted.

(iv) Hungary
European Community operators may carry goods to, from and through Hungary and may enter the country with an empty vehicle in order to collect a return load. Third country loads are permitted as long as they are included in the terms of bilateral agreements between the three countries. Cabotage is not permitted.

Permits are required for certain operations. Own account operators do not require permits but must carry an own account declaration. Hire and reward operators do require permits except in respect of certain exempt traffic.

Generally speaking Hungary operates the much repressive permit arrangements in Eastern Europe. However, unlike the DDR or Romania (as we shall see) the permit arrangements are fairly and honestly applied, and there are no hidden biases towards domestic operators.

European Community operators do not have to pay additional taxes in Hungary. The one exception to this is in the case of overweight vehicles - when a single axle is over ten tons; or a double axle over sixteen tons. Notably, fees are payable in local currency (forints) and not a convertible currency.

Western vehicle spares are available from very selected locations, often only through the national hauliers Hungarocamion or Volan. Non Hungarian vehicles can only obtain fuel using coupons. Both spares and fuel are available only for convertible currency. All fines and repair bills are payable only in convertible currency. Other requirements are for a full passport, an international driving licence, a Green Card and vehicle registration document.

(v) Poland

Poland represents the simplest case for all European Community operators in the Eastern Bloc, partly because of the creation of the convertible zloty from 1 January 1990. EC operators may carry goods to, from or through Poland and may enter Poland with an empty vehicle to collect a return load. Third party traffic is allowed, subject to bilateral agreements between all parties, but cabotage is prohibited. No permits are required.

Various documents are required:

- Green Card;
- a vehicle registration document;
- passport;
- visa and an international driving licence.

Polish national driving hours are applicable but these tend to be more lenient than those of the European Community. No additional taxes for foreign vehicles are applied.

Western vehicle spares are unobtainable, but payment for fuel, maintenance, repairs or any spares that are obtained can be made either in local or convertible currency, and (normally) at local rates.

(vi) Romania

European Community operators may carry loads to, from or through Romania and may enter the country in order to collect a return load. Third party and cabotage traffic are prohibited. Permits are not required for any operations representing, theoretically, an extremely liberal policy towards international road haulage. Practice differs drastically from this, and Western operation in Romania is both very rare, and fraught with problems.

A variety of regulations have to be recognised - the vehicle registration document must be carried plus a full driving licence, passport and visa. TIR carnets are accepted, and national driving hours legislation is applied, but is generally as lenient as that of the EC.

Taxation is only imposed on EC vehicles entering Romania if vehicles exceed a variety of maximum weights and dimensions. A full tank of fuel may be imported duty free.

Romania is renowned for a theoretically liberal administrative policy in relation to international hauliers from the West, but one which in practice has been corrupt, and remains financially harsh. Services of all types are available only for hard currency and at penal rates of exchange. Spares for vehicles (including Romanian!) are largely unobtainable. Imports from Austria are very expensive and slow. Road conditions are dreadful (narrow and potholed), lighting poor or non-existent even in cities. All subsistence (food and accommodation) has to be paid in hard currency. There are harsh penalties for those involved in accidents or who commit traffic offences. Diesel fuel, of low quality, is only available using coupons purchased with hard currency.

Overall, despite revolutionary changes during 1989/90, the position for Western hauliers remains depressing. Even the supposed liberal regime allowing free competition unhindered by permit arrangements, is manipulated to ensure Romtrans (the Romanian State haulier) retains almost all the traffic.

Conclusions

Thus, the structure of European Community hauliers, operating in the Eastern Bloc, has been outlined above. A number of significant issues should emerge:

-    that of convertible currency. In the majority of cases, European Community hauliers have to purchase fuel, spares, maintenance, accommodation and so on, in convertible currency, often at penal rates. National hauliers are not faced with these same constraints (or prices resulting);

-    administrative bias. Many Eastern European countries appear to operate liberal policies towards international hauliers, but in practice bias all procedures/policies towards their own fleets, thus exacerbating the problems caused by the convertible currency regulations;

- the lack of facilities for Western operators including difficulties of obtaining spares, and maintenance facilities. This is in spite of the fact that all East European State hauliers (except Romania) operate Western made vehicles and have the facilities and spares for them readily available. Only Hungary really shows any commercial appreciation of the opportunities available in this market.

It is also notable how administratively complex the whole system of international road transport has become, with separate bilateral agreements for each pair of countries to which each operator is bound as he/she passes through a country, coupled with a number of international conventions which also apply (for example TIR, ATP etc). Within the European Community such complexities are being reduced but there are no signs of improvement with respect to the East European countries.

In practice the conditions for Eastern Bloc operators entering the EC space in EC-CMEA trade are different in two ways than that for EC operators entering the CMEA area.

(i)   The convertible currency issue does not apply in the same way. In the East, two currency regimes apply (hard currency, Western hauliers; soft currency, Eastern Bloc hauliers) and commonly, therefore, two sets of prices.

(ii)   Subsidy and State ownership, still dominant in the Eastern Bloc, providing preferential commercial treatment to Eastern European hauliers, over their West European counter- parts.

In theoretical and administrative terms there are few differences, as TIR rules, bilateral agreements and the like apply equally to each group in each area. In later sections we shall go on to examine the ways the CMEA country operations are managed, controlled and financed, to establish the level of disharmony that exists between the East and West in the international road haulage market.

One final issue should be noted at this stage, however. Despite relatively mammoth changes in political, social and economic structures during 1989 and 1990, commercial practice, particularly in the road haulage market, has yet to change to any considerable extent. The old structures of State ownership remain in Hungary, Bulgaria, Romania and

TABLE 2 : CMEA INDEBTEDNESS

A. ESTIMATED GROSS HARD CURRENCY DEBT

				$ (billion)	
COUNTRY	**1984**	**1985**	**1986**	**1987**	**1988**
Bulgaria	2.1	3.5	4.9	6.2	6.8
Czechoslovakia	3.1	3.3	4.0	5.0	5.6
GDR	11.6	13.5	16.1	18.9	18.6
Hungary	8.8	11.8	15.1	17.7	17.2
Poland	26.9	29.7	33.5	39.2	39.1
Romania	7.2	6.6	6.4	5.7	4.0
USSR	22.1	31.4	37.5	41.8	41.9
TOTAL	81.8	99.8	117.5	134.5	133.2

B. GROSS LIABILITIES TO BIS REPORTING BANKS (i)

				$ (billion)	
COUNTRY	**Dec 1984**	**Dec 1985**	**Dec 1986**	**Dec 1987**	**Dec 1988**
Bulgaria	1.6	2.9	4.1	5.4	5.6
Czechoslovakia	2.4	2.7	3.1	4.2	4.5
GDR (ii)	8.3	10.3	12.0	14.1	15.6
Hungary	6.8	8.6	10.0	12.4	11.5
Poland	9.0	10.2	11.0	12.3	10.6
Romania	3.8	3.0	2.9	2.5	0.8
USSR	16.4	22.6	29.4	33.3	36.8
TOTAL	48.3	60.3	72.5	84.2	86.7

(i)   Banks in the Group of ten countries plus Austria, Bahamas, Bahrain, Cayman Islands, Denmark, Finland, Hong Kong, Ireland, Luxembourg, Netherlands, Antilles, Norway, Panama, Singapore, Spain and Switzerland.

(ii) Excludes lending by FRG banks to GDR.

Source : East European Trade Council

3 CMEA trade with the European Community

The CMEA Structure

The Council for Mutual Economic Assistance (CMEA), or colloquially 'Comecon', was established in January 1949 in Moscow, where its headquarters remain. Its original members were the Soviet Union, Bulgaria, Czechoslovakia, Hungary, Poland and Romania. Albania joined shortly after and the DDR was accepted in September 1950. Since then Cuba, Mongolia and Vietnam have joined as associate members; whilst Albania have now left. Yugoslavia joined as an associate member.

The main motivator behind the creation of the CMEA was the Soviet Union, who remain to this day the dominant influence. The main objective originally was an attempt to counter the effects of the 1947 Marshall Plan through which the USA had offered financial aid to both Western Europe and the Eastern Bloc to overcome the ravages of World War II. The Soviet Union rejected this aid and compelled Czechoslovakia and Poland, which had already accepted, to reverse their decisions. The establishment of the CMEA also provided an East European response to the Organisation for European Economic Co-operation (OEEC) that was set up to co-ordinate the distribution of Marshall Plan funds in Western Europe, to liberalise trade and to help in improving the international payment system amongst West European States.

Because of the fundamental difference in West and East European economic systems the CMEA's functions differed from those of the OEEC. The CMEA's major tasks were the exchange of economic experience between Members, co-ordination of foreign trade, extension of technical aid to one another, and rendering mutual assistance with respect to raw materials, foodstuffs, machinery and other items (Feld, 1984).

For the Soviet Union the underlying reasons for the creation of the CMEA were both political and economic. It provided an instrument of control over East European economies and ensured that the Soviet model would be applied to political, social and economic life. A combination of economic and military Soviet domination ensured compliance at the time the CMEA was founded and, of course, since then until fairly recent events.

On establishment, no constitution was produced but, instead, a policy statement was issued which served as a substitute until 1960. It emphasised the principle of sovereignty, protecting at least in theory, the freedom of action and independence of the East European member states - although clearly still subject to substantial economic and political pressure. The principle of sovereignty, although clearly rather diluted by Soviet dominance, has actually been exercised on a (limited) number of occasions. Unanimity is (and always has been) required for all CMEA decisions, a principle that has been adhered to. For example, in 1962 Poland and the Soviet Union proposed converting the CMEA into a unified planning organ empowered to impose common plans and organisations; it was rejected by Romania alone, on the grounds that it would turn the CMEA into a supra-national body. This protection of sovereignty is a major difference from the direction in which the European Community is heading.

With this strong insistence on national freedom within the CMEA structure, progress economically has been far slower than that of the European community. However, to a large extent this is also a consequence of the difference in economic systems between East and West.

Due to the principle of nationalisation and State ownership which underlies CMEA economic, social and political objectives, the only form of integration between member states has been the 'co-ordination of plans' and the 'division of international socialist labour'.

Plan co-ordination was introduced from 1962 and involves the production of plans for the various sectors of the CMEA economy - for example, iron and steel, or chemicals - from which individual, national production plans can be developed. Within each country plans for individual plants can then be produced which dictate the level of service provision (including transport) that is needed.

In some more detail (and taking the transport service sector as an example), four basic levels of planning can be identified within the Eastern Bloc until recent changes in some states, moving from the broadest to the most specific - that is, applied directly by the CMEA, to that applied to an industrial plant or service. Theoretically, and practically as far as has been possible, these plans were co-ordinated with the more specific derived from the more strategic.

(i)   Long range plans were essentially those of a strategic level and covered periods in excess of ten years, particularly involving investment planning throughout the CMEA area. Since plans were derived for the CMEA area as a whole and for each Eastern European country within the CMEA, transport featured as a subordinate part of two main long-range plan issues:

-       that of determining the rate and direction of economic development within the area concerned; and
-       that of the development of infrastructure.

More detailed transport requirements derived from these broader strategic economic objectives.

The transport elements of the long-range plans were prepared by the transport sectors of special commissions formed of state planners, academics and executives. They were derived in close consultation with planners in other economic sectors, including the national economies as a whole, and with strategic CMEA planners. Maximum time spans were normally ten to fifteen years, precluding precise indicators and providing merely a strategy for transport development in the freight and passenger sectors.

(ii)   Multi-year plans for transport were derived from economic plans based previously on the directives on the national Communist Party, and still on the Councils of Ministers. Predictions were based on the assumed needs of industry given the industrial development plan, and to a lesser extent, with a lower priority, the needs of passenger mobility. In more detail, specific industrial sectors predicted future demand based on past experience of transport needs and future estimates of production targets. Different industrial products require different transport facilities and services and national plans for production of each commodity are used to decide upon transport investments. These transport investment plans related both to infrastructure (rail links, highways, airports etc) and equipment (trucks, railcars etc).

(iii)   Annual plans for each Eastern European countrywere developed in more detail once again with predictions made of the specific routes and modes to be used for each product. Investment and service provision then followed to meet projected demand. Regional inputs were important here as plans for transport requirements become specific. These plans were revised annually to meet changing production levels.

(iv)   Operative plans were designed for quarterly and monthly periods, reflecting very short term service provision that was considered rather than investment policy. Thus the focus of attention was more the timetabling of services and the provision of vehicles than the quantity and quality of infrastructure. Details of loadings of freight and passenger were compared with those of planned service provision and the latter adapted, where possible, to individual needs.

Overall, the 'planned' approach was complex, rigid and constrained flexibility. It was bureaucratically inefficient and required constant discussion between its strategic, regional and national levels and industry to meet fluctuations in plan objectives, and actual industrial production in terms of freight and passenger loadings. More specific drawbacks include:

(i)   Failure to co-ordinate the levels of planning noted above, and that of industrial production and transport investment and operation, despite the fact that this is the prime reason for such

25

planning. This co-ordination breakdown was noted by Gumpel (1967), and attempts to overcome these problems have been made by individual countries, including the establishment of a National Transport Complex in Bulgaria in 1974.

(ii)   Transport planning is in terms of physical quantities with few (if any) measures of efficiency used. To quote Mieczkowski (1980),
"... there is no planned economic co-ordination of transport; rather, there is only 'exante' administration of transport".

(iii)   Transport remains subordinate to economic growth, having to react rapidly (and frequently failing) to changes in industrial plans, and to failures to keep to industrial targets. Transport planning is based upon industrial data from a previous period rather than reliable industrial plans for future economic activity.

(iv)   The CMEA continues to fail to produce its own Common Transport Policy (c.f. the European Community). So far only partial co-ordination has been attempted as well as organisational and technical co-operation and joint work on individual projects. One major problem has been the failure to gain true co-operation between national plans for the Eastern European area.

(v)   The failure to develop investment appraisal methodologies based on efficiency measures has inhibited planning of the transport sector. The inadequacies of welfare economic or related methodologies in the light of Eastern European policy requirements (which, for example, preclude the use of interest rates as a basis for investment appraisal) makes planning very difficult.

Another related problem is the failure to derive standard methods of measuring efficiency for the transport sector, either between modes or between nations in the eastern Bloc, thus making meaningful comparisons difficult if not impossible.

These problems are widely recognised within the CMEA Countries and attempts, as noted earlier, are being made to rationalise pricing policies and structures. The efforts expended on complex planning is nothing short of prodigious and overbearing. The introduction of 'scientific'

26

planning rules have been applied to some problems, but overall 'command' planning for transport remains rigid and inflexible whilst omitting serious issues, notably that of an effective investment appraisal methodology.

As a final indictment, such planning has failed to eliminate wastage in countries where economic resources are in short supply. To quote Mieczkowski (1980):

"Unnecessary haulage takes place on a staggering scale and cost consciousness reveals extensive blind spots".

In terms of the 'division of international socialist labour', the CMEA ambition was one of allocating production between countries according to efficiency of production. Thus car components are produced in a number of East European countries for the Lada/Moskvitch which are then assembled in Bulgaria and the Soviet Union. However, nationalism and political tensions have reduced the level of co-operation below that which might have been expected.

Major joint projects are also promoted with rather more success than has been achieved through the planning process or division of labour. Examples include the Moscow-Baltic highway, the USSR-Bulgaria gas pipeline and the USSR-DDR/Poland/Hungary oil pipeline (Friendship Line).

The CMEA has been a major influence on economic development in the East - controlling integration, allocating production, producing long-range plans to be adopted nationally and thus dictating the direction of industrial and commercial development. Inevitably, this includes an impact on transport and more specifically international transport, particularly from the point of view of servicing import and export requirements and the construction of international road vehicles. Indirectly, by dictating industrial development and pricing policies for hard currency acquisition, it has affected markets for products and thus their distribution needs. Also it has provided a mechanism for integration of international road transport although this has been little used, with national fleets tending to serve their own markets and those of imports and exports to and from the West.

In the years since 1988, a number of notable events have occurred which have affected, and will continue to markedly affect, CMEA activities:

(i)   In June 1988, an agreement of mutual recognition and economic co-operation was signed between the EC and CMEA institutions which should lead to the promotion of trading relations. Prior to this, the existence of the EC had not been recognised by the CMEA.

(ii)   The currency of Poland is now largely convertible helping to improve trade relations between Poland and other nations, despite the domestic hardship involved. In the climate of change in Eastern Europe further convertibility is likely in the next few years. For those countries still with unconvertible currencies - the Soviet Union, Bulgaria, Czechoslovakia, Hungary and Romania - all external trade with the west must be conducted using earned hard currency which is in short supply, counter- trade, bartering, licensing or through joint ventures.

(iii)   Calls for the disbanding of the CMEA have now been made, both within and without East Europe. With the dismembering of the Communist Party and its influence, and the rise of alternatives to Socialism, the role of the CMEA has been questioned. Certainly, the introduction of market economics and the decline of international Socialism, has made command planning an anachronism.

(v)   From 1 January 1991, all intra CMEA trade will be in convertible currency, eliminating the trade in 'transferable roubles' and barter that used to characterise the CMEA. This places even greater demands on the short supply of hard currency available to the Eastern Bloc, through selling their goods and services to the West.

State Trading Nations - their role

So far we have seen that the CMEA has set the basic planned framework for the Eastern Bloc countries, within which each country provides short term plans which dictate industrial production and service provision (including transport). Transport is thus seen as a service dictated to by industrial production needs - and investment is directed accordingly. International road transport is part of that service need, but as we shall see, differs notably from domestic transport services in its objectives and operations.

28

In terms of the organisation of foreign trade, in various degrees decentralising reforms have been progressing in East Europe since the mid 1980's, and in the last year have increased dramatically. In most of East Europe the State monopoly of foreign trade, as was prevalent before the mid 1980's, is gradually being replaced by increasing numbers of enterprises permitted to conduct foreign trade on their own account. The details for each CMEA country being covered will be noted in the appropriate section. However, whereas in the past the power to spend hare currency was centrally controlled by means of the State planning procedures, the tendency now is for only major infrastructure projects to be State financed, whilst more and more organisations obtain direct foreign trading rights as long, of course, as they have the hard currency to do it. In future, these organisations will have to operate on a profit or loss, self financing basis. This includes many of the international road haulage organisations - especially Pekaes (Poland), Hungarocamion (Hungary) and Cesmad (Czechoslovakia).

In reality, in 1990, the FTO's and State Ministries retain substantial control (total in Romania) and are the only bodies with the experience of foreign trade activities. Hence, it will be a long time before independent foreign trading is truly achieved.

There are a number of ways in which foreign trade is financed, largely stimulated by the shortage of convertible currency. Thus, for example, an international road haulier in the East wishing to invest in West European vehicles, or an Eastern Bloc company wishing to develop a truck construction industry, can take any one of a number of financial routes to pay for their acquisitions:

(i) <u>Cash or Credit</u>
A large proportion of East/West trade is carried out in a similar manner to exporting to other parts of the world, that is, payment is either arranged on 'Cash against Documents' (cash being hard or Western currency) terms or on a Letter of Credit, Supplier Credit or Buyer Credit basis. A number of 'lines of credit' guaranteed by ECGD have been extended by British banks in Eastern Europe, covering individual projects and the supply of capital goods as well as 'shopping basket' arrangements.

(ii) Barter Trade
Exchange of goods, usually of equivalent total value, thus eliminating the use of currency. A type of trade popular in the past when industrial gods were paid for by the supply of commodities, such as tomatoes, chemicals, jam etc. The commodities are then often side-tracked to a 'barter or counter-trade dealer'. This type of transaction is now much less common.

(iii) Switch-trading
Payment for goods exported to an East European country is received in hard currency from a third country, the latter having a negative balance with the East European country. This is the most simple case. Switch-deals are often far more complicated.

(iv) Counter-purchase
A Western exporter is requested to purchase East European goods, (more likely to be industrial items rather than commodities) usually equal to a percentage of the value of the exports to the East European partner. Normally two separate contracts are involved. The percentage of the contract value to be taken in counter-trade varies from 10% to 100% or more, depending on many factors such as flexibility of individual East European enterprises, urgency of import, trade balance between countries, etc. The penalty to be paid from failure to complete counter-trade obligations also varies. The goods offered in counter-purchase are not normally directly related to the industrial goods being exported by the Western partner.

(v) Compensation/Buy-back
This is one of the forms of trade currently favoured by the CMEA. Basically, the Western partner is required to supply technology know-how, and often equipment and installation/training work force, thus providing the East European partner with a plant producing a form of product possibly new to that country.

Initial financing is arranged with a Western bank, but the repayment burden is eased by the Western partner's obligation to purchase the product from the plant to the value of 100% of the project cost (perhaps more, to cover interest payments on the initial credit), thus assisting the East European partner to earn valuable hard currency and in some cases establishing/testing a Western market for the product.

Unlike most counter-trade, these compensation/buy-back deals involve a long period, five to fifteen years, as the plant has to be built and commissioned before payment in product can be made. Complex pricing agreements have to be worked out to forestall a change in either market demand or price for the product when it eventually appears.

These forms of self-financing deals are particularly popular when a project is outside the Five Year Plan and thus unbudgeted.

(vi) Licensing

Is popular in Eastern Europe, partly due to the savings in development time and cost, and also as a means of rapidly updating local technology and thus achieving targets set out in FYP's. Payment is usually in the form of a one-off lump sum; royalty arrangements are less common, probably due to uncertainty regarding production schedules. In some instances, especially where there is some form of co-operation or technology updating agreement, payment may be made in goods. In many licensing operations, apart from the FTO and 'end-user', a specialist state licensing organisation is involved in the negotiations.

(vii) Joint Ventures

This is perhaps the most sophisticated form of co-operation and involves equity and/or know-how investment by the Western partner in a joint company with an East European organisation either in the West (normally a joint marketing company for East European products) or in individual CMEA countries for co-production purposes. Over recent years the East Europeans have become increasingly keen to promote joint venture arrangements and updated or, as in the case of the Soviet Union and the DDR, new legislation has been published in every country. However, the appeal of joint ventures is often far greater to an East European partner, motivated by the urgent need to acquire new technology without committing scarce hard currency reserves, than it is to the Western partner.

A number of examples already exist in the East European transport market - including UPS (Parcels) and Sovtransauto (Moscow); UPS and Polish Airports Authority in Warsaw and Krakow, Poland; and TNT with Aeroflot in Moscow, and Malev in Budapest.

The significance of these finance deals to international road haulage is that they influence pricing, operating and management policies in the East - and thus affect the market for East-West trade for transport as a whole. We shall return to this issue later.

The Structure of Transport Organisation in the Eastern Bloc

Here, we shall deal only with the traditional structure of transport organisation in Eastern Europe, and will look at the detail of individual national structures at a later stage. Due to the influence of the CMEA and the political and economic domination of the Soviet Union in the past, the organisation of transport is remarkably consistent throughout Eastern Europe.

The highest authority directly concerned with transport is normally the Ministry of Transport which receives instructions from the Council of Ministers/Parliament/ Communist Party. The Ministry normally translates the impacts of the planned economy into plans for the individual transport sections who in turn serve the production units and retailers (for freight), and passengers.

Decisions for investment (for example in new vehicles) are made by the Ministry in line with demands from industry as determined by the planning system. Sometimes, transport capacity constraints will in turn restrict industrial production so that the two sides of the equation match. This occurs when investment is impossible or likely to be inadequate for any reason.

Beneath the Ministry is normally a series of enterprises actually involved in transport operations.

Conventionally these enterprises can be divided into:
road freight	-	local urban transport
		regional transport international transport
road passenger	-	urban passenger
		regional transport
rail freight	-	national
		international
rail passenger	-	national, suburban
		metro services

32

```
water freight      -      coastal/national
                          international
air freight        -      international
air passenger      -      national
                          international
```

As we are concerned with the international road freight sector, we shall concentrate on road freight organisation alone.

Generally, there would be road freight enterprises set up for each district/county, responsible for local distribution of freight to industry and retailers. These would operate between industrial producers, railheads or freight transhipment points within a county area, and commonly utilise relatively small, East European made, trucks and drawbar trailers. Competition between operators is still rare as they are normally state owned with benefits supposedly coming from economies of scale, integration and co-ordinated planning. Such operators include Transcom (Romania) - a State monopoly; and Volan (Hungary) and PKS (Poland), both oligopolies.

Regional road freight transport remains uncommon. Journeys of 20-40 km (dependent on country) are believed to be uneconomic by road except under special circumstances (eg no rail link), and traffic has been normally directed to the railways - this still frequently occurs. Separate enterprises sometimes exist to provide regional road transport services, but frequently hire/lease local delivery trucks from country/district companies.

International haulage is a totally separate concern in Poland, Hungary, Romania and Bulgaria, but is not so in Czechoslovakia where national and international fleets are intermixed. Fleets are commonly Western made (excepting Romania) or at least dominated. It is operated under broad control from the Ministry either directly (eg Romania) or indirectly through direction of traffic, and demands and controls for hard currency. Eastern European international hauliers are Pekaes (Poland), Hungarocamion (Hungary), Cesmad (Czechoslovakia), Somat (Bulgaria) and VEB Deutrans (DDR) - each is a semi or complete monopoly.

However, outside of this state controlled transport organisation there are a large proportion of vehicles (in Romania 70%) run by industrial State companies and Ministries for specific products - for example, building materials, coal and chemicals. In the past these fleets were not allowed to be utilised by other sectors, but increasingly this is changing. Such vehicles are only occasionally used for international transport.

Many things in national and international road haulage are beginning to change in Eastern Europe, in particular the role of competition and the independence of FTO's and hauliers to choose how to price, invest and so on. However, due to the factors of economic inertia, inexperience and financial constraints, many of the old systems and methods will remain as they have operated for some time yet.

To summarise the international road haulage sector, most East European countries operate State owned fleets of Western made vehicles, which have a near or absolute monopoly of international road freight transport. The organisation is still largely controlled by the State Ministry, and has to operate in line with State objectives - and long term CMEA plans. The main objective of such fleets is to retain a high share of East European based traffic to earn hard currency. Such earnings are commonly returned to the State who then allow a proportion to be returned to the operator for re-investment. A typical structure for freight transport organisation in Eastern Europe is given Figure 1. The detailed variations for each country will be outlined in the relevant sections of this report.

Modal choice, once the sole concern of the State Ministry, is now a rather more flexible issue in all the Eastern European countries - but economic geography often dictates that there is little choice at all. Thus the majority of long distance movements over 40 km still travel by rail, whilst only local deliveries between transhipment points and retailers (for example) are road carried. The concept of speed and accuracy in delivery time and care for products are still alien and subservient to that of theoretical macro efficiency in the transport sector. Time will change this, inevitably as the Eastern Bloc becomes more market orientated.

Until recently all freight forwarding into and out of each Eastern Bloc country was totally controlled by the State through its Foreign Trade Organisations. Freight movements organised outside of these organisations were illegal. In recent years this has begun to change, and it is common now in Poland and Hungary for industries to avoid the State FTO's and organise their own transport. However, the FTO's still organise the majority of trade in all of the Eastern Bloc countries, and in Romania are the only groups entitled to do so.

34

However, where competition and freedom of choice has been encouraged, then it will undoubtedly have some effect on modal choice, and the conditions of trade, previously dictated almost entirely by the East European partner. The best example of change comes from Poland, where previously all transport had to be organised through the State freight forwarder, Hartwig, whereas now any organisation can be used, including Western groups, private Polish independents, or the industry itself.

Some Conclusions

Things are changing in Eastern Europe. Political reform is evident throughout the European CMEA area. All CMEA countries were party to an agreement signed in Sofia on 26 January 1990, that the CMEA was to change over by 1 January 1991 to a market system based on convertible currencies and away from barter and the notorious transferable rouble. The pace of actual reform varies considerably between nations from the hectic in the DDR, to the orderly but reasonably fast in Poland and Hungary, to the slow and ponderous in Bulgaria, and the chaotic in Romania.

It is almost impossible to predict the next moves, and consequently, their effect on the transport market. We can, however, identify four trends which will be significant and which will affect the pace of change and its ultimate success:

(i)   the ability of the West, and particularly the European Community, to aid the process of change, involving financial, economic and social/political assistance. Clearly the amount and type of aid will be instrumental in affecting detailed national transport policies and in particular those for international road haulage;

(ii)   the issue of German reunification and its economic impact on the rest of Eastern Europe;

(iii)   opposition to change from both those previously in leading positions in bureaucracies of the Communist Party who enjoy (still) many privileges, and parts of the 'working population' who are likely to face lowering living standards as economic restructuring takes place;

35

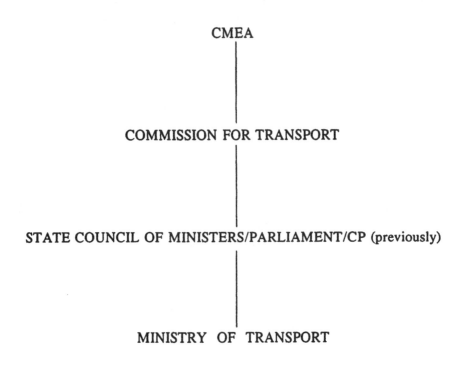

CMEA

COMMISSION FOR TRANSPORT

STATE COUNCIL OF MINISTERS/PARLIAMENT/CP (previously)

MINISTRY OF TRANSPORT

Local road freight.	Regional road freight.	International
Organised by county operating local deliveries within counties. (Max 20-40 km)	Usually using local vehicles. Inter country movements when necessary.	Normally a separate company operating own vehicles.

FIGURE 1 : TYPICAL ROAD FREIGHT ORGANISATION
                IN THE CMEA

(iv)   the greater freedom of expression and movement which has created growing and possibly unrealistic expectations for the future.

To quote the National Westminster Bank Review of 1989:

"Whilst political reform can be achieved relatively quickly, industrial and economic reform is rather more uncertain, takes longer to implement and tends to exacerbate short-term political difficulties.   Much of the industrial structure of Eastern Europe is very backward, inefficient, and therefore unable to compete effectively in free world markets.   Internal pressure to raise living standards will be strong and it is likely that, for even the minimum requirements of the local populations to be met, some assistance will need to be provided by the West.   However, it is important to stress that Western assistance is secondary to the internal reform programme.   Such assistance could be wasted unless it is linked (through, say, the IMF) to specific and often painful recovery measures. Initially, the requirement is likely to be for access to Western support to fund higher domestic consumption of imported goods.   Clearly, in the aftermath of the Latin American debt problem, the bulk of such balance of payments support will only be provided by Western governments, whose decision will depend on wider political and strategic considerations.   Private financial institutions can play a role, but must ultimately be guided by commercial considerations.

In the longer term, investment flows, and technology and managerial transfers will be needed to restructure industry.   The restructuring process will be painful. It must include the reduction of subsidies, which will raise prices; the closure of inefficient factories and industries, which will lead to high, and possibly very concentrated, unemployment; and the sterilising of huge domestic monetary overhangs.   Even when investment has commercial attractions it seems realistic to assume that the finance will not be forthcoming unless Western governments provide suitable guarantees.

It is not at all clear that the price of substantial economic reform will be acceptable throughout Eastern Europe.   The current euphoria over increasing political freedoms may yet be replaced by a more cautious outlook, as the costs and realities of reform begin to appear. Substantial moves towards more efficient market-regulated production will inevitably entail   sharply   higher   prices   and   a   more   rational   use   of resources. In particular, the security of full employment will disappear, and substantial unemployment will become a prolonged feature of structural reform. Whilst difficult to calculate, overall unemployment in many economies may rise to 20% or more, with substantially higher rates applying in particular regions.

None of the East European countries has sufficient financial resources to finance major unemployment for any length of time. Whilst in the short and medium term the move toward market orientated systems will benefit many of the local populations, there will be some, particularly amongst the existing poor and unskilled, for whom the outlook is bleak. It may well be that for many, a reformed communist system will be preferable to full blooded capitalism, with its connotations of winners and losers.

It is far too early to predict with authority which East European countries are most likely to succeed in their economic reforms. Although much will depend on the assistance received from outside Comecon, the key to success remains the ability to take bold, but sometimes painful decisions. The most likely success is the GDR, because of the prospective assistance available from the Federal Republic.

Czechoslovakia may well manage better than many of its neighbours the new political and economic challenges, whilst in the Soviet Union, the retention of one party communist rule may, paradoxically, enable economic changes to succeed because it will add to stability. The potential threat posed by a destabilised and impoverished Soviet Union is likely to produce significant Western assistance to a resource-rich economy with a relatively low level of foreign debt, though the burden is growing. The outlook for both Poland and Hungary is in many ways less optimistic. Both are already burdened with crippling hard currency debts, with Poland widely regarded as being insolvent, and Hungary, if not insolvent, is highly illiquid. Bulgaria is some way behind other East European countries in its approach to reform, whilst Romania, following the removal of the Ceaucescu regime, is in a state of economic, political and social chaos".

All this will affect transport as a major service to industry, and international transport perhaps in particular. It will have to become market orientated, more competitive with Western hauliers, and yet will have to restructure itself to accommodate reduced subsidies and new organisational requirements, whilst national economies deteriorate. Internal road freight markets will not provide much of an alternative to international work, as economies decline and stagnate.

East European indebtedness to the West is another issue that will have an impact on East-West trade and subsequently international road freight. It is inevitable that economic reforms in Eastern Europe will require substantial financial assistance from the West, some of which will be in the form of loans. Onerous levels of debt already exist (Table 2).

Whilst calculations of GDP in Eastern Europe vary widely, absolute debt burdens (a test of solvency) range from slight, at under 5% of GDP in Czechoslovakia, Romania and the USSR, to onerous in Poland at 57%, and Hungary at 67%. Total debt service ratios, (a test of liquidity), range from 16% in Czechoslovakia and 21% in the Soviet Union, to over 40% in the GDR, Hungary and Poland, at which level debt servicing costs are burdensome. Idiosyncratic Romania is prepaying debt and, despite apparently high current ratios, will have virtually no debt outstanding by mid-1990. Any substantial future commercial borrowing by many East European countries will quickly raise debt burdens to levels which have proved unsustainable elsewhere in the world unless dramatic hard currency export growth can be achieved.

Consequently, the economic reforms necessary will either fail or will cause at the best, short term commercial and social hardships with obvious ramifications for the international transport market.

Given the changes that are taking place and the crippling problems facing Eastern European economies, it should be explained that few East European countries have yet markedly altered the structures for transport provision and organisation, and its objectives (eg hard currency earnings). The State's involvement in international road transport remains high even in Poland, where it is most liberated and especially in Romania and Bulgaria where no retreat has been made. The same personnel continue to work in a partly changed environment with little training back up to provide the basis for adaptation to new objectives and no experience of the new ground rules.

Tables 3-8 give an indication of levels of imports and exports to and from the six Eastern Bloc countries of the CMEA and the EC between 1982 and 1988. The statistics presented here have to be treated with care and suspicion as a number of them are unreliable. Romania, in particular, was renowned for inventing statistics to match plan objectives set by Ceausescu and his followers. It is not the intention here, to analyse the data in any detail, merely to draw out a few trends and to indicate their relevance to the international trucking market:

(i)   The growth in trade generally, between the EC and the Eastern Bloc even before the recent political and economic changes which have caused short term chaos, but long term, will provide a major incentive to increasing trade. Notable exceptions to this growth are Romanian imports from the EC which under the Ceausescu dynasty declined substantially, as part of the overall deliberate policy of reducing indebted- ness to the west. This policy has now been largely reversed and more recent statistics for 1990 reflect an upturn in EC-Romanian trade.

(ii)   The substantial growth in certain specific trades - especially Bulgarian, Czechoslovakian and Polish imports from the EC and Czechoslovakian, Hungarian and Polish exports to the EC.

(iii)   Both these trends suggest increasing transport demand - and with the growth of imports to the EC more suited to road freight, and with increasing congestion on East European railways there will be a marked increase in demand for international road haulage.

(iv)   Table 9 gives added, if incomplete, emphasis to the growth in road traffic carrying freight. There is massive growth in road transported freight entering the DDR and Hungary, and larger increases in exports from Czechoslovakia, the DDR, Hungary and Poland. Data is unavailable for Bulgaria and Romania. A figure that also should be noted, is the massive growth in road freight transitting Hungary.

TABLE 3 : CMEA - EC TRADE
BULGARIA 1982-1988

BULGARIA   EXPORTS (from)   IMPORTS (to)

(m US $)

	EXPORTS (from)							IMPORTS (to)						
	1982	1983	1984	1985	1986	1987	1988	1982	1983	1984	1985	1986	1987	1988
Belgium-Lux	24.7	21.7	16.9	17.3	19.9	15.6	18.5	50.1	54.7	51.6	67.1	62.0	90.2	87.6
Denmark	8.9	3.8	3.5	4.3	5.0	4.4	4.1	·8.1	16.1	13.4	12.4	15.4	16.1	17.6
France	92.2	62.1	50.3	53.0	65.8	63.2	56.4	116.5	122.0	114.3	182.6	139.8	141.9	167.9
GFR	176.4	159.9	137.1	147.3	168.0	179.7	166.2	551.2	536.8	517.4	624.4	856.1	963.5	980.9
Eire	0.6	0.8	1.2	0.9	0.8	3.0	1.1	3.0	2.2	2.3	5.9	7.1	4.2	11.3
Italy	106.9	91.3	72.6	76.4	87.9	94.3	101.2	177.3	128.2	151.0	184.7	214.8	233.1	224.2
Netherlands	18.5	14.0	19.9	32.0	31.4	39.9	31.7	52.6	85.0	46.6	49.6	72.2	83.4	92.5
Spain	15.2	39.3	36.1	45.1	46.4	44.7	46.3	32.0	42.0	48.6	50.1	32.9	101.6	38.0
UK	33.0	17.0	20.6	26.2	43.2	36.2	45.4	88.6	74.2	81.9	161.8	140.4	162.8	161.3
Greece	78.9	59.9	45.8	29.8	31.0	65.4	78.4	48.5	47.9	46.6	49.0	64.0	46.7	56.0
Portugal	1.5	0.9	1.5	1.8	4.8	30.3	5.6	6.4	5.3	5.2	5.2	4.1	10.7	6.9
Σ EC	556.8	470.7	405.4	434.0	504.2	576.6	554.9	1134.3	1114.4	1078.8	1392.7	1608.6	1854.1	1844.6
Σ World	2068.6	1979.0	1906.3	2007.5	2002.3	2236.3	2457.2	2987.9	3103.5	3017.1	3464.0	3728.7	4182.6	4460.1

(excluding USSR and other non-members)
(ie, Alb, Cuba, Cz, DDR, Mon, Nk)

Source : Direction of Trade Statistics Yearbook 1989 IMF

TABLE 4 : CMEA - EC TRADE
CZECHOSLOVAKIA 1982-1988

CZECHOSLOVAKIA

(m US $)

EXPORTS (from)

	1982	1983	1984	1985	1986	1987	1988
Belgium-Lux	49.9	49.8	49.5	50.9	67.4	76.1	84.6
Denmark	56.1	53.9	62.5	61.5	65.6	65.4	61.8
France	156.7	142.7	143.4	145.1	182.8	207.6	225.9
GFR	768.4	787.4	763.3	780.8	925.0	1068.4	1138.6
Eire	9.7	8.7	10.9	11.6	12.1	10.2	15.1
Italy	226.8	203.7	196.1	199.0	234.6	260.6	305.3
Netherlands	116.8	101.5	111.6	108.4	143.7	150.6	145.5
Spain	26.9	26.8	29.0	34.2	46.4	54.2	70.8
UK	131.7	138.7	139.5	139.0	167.1	211.3	263.4
Greece	34.8	30.3	38.3	45.1	50.0	59.1	70.9
Portugal	8.6	5.5	13.9	6.9	9.1	14.6	13.5
Σ EC	1586.5	1549.1	1557.9	1582.4	1903.9	2178.1	2395.3
Σ World	5537.7	5390.7	5281.7	5335.4	5900.0	6587.5	7354.6

IMPORTS (to)

	1982	1983	1984	1985	1986	1987	1988
Belgium-Lux	69.2	67.6	63.3	69.3	100.8	99.8	100.4
Denmark	26.9	26.1	36.9	32.2	47.8	54.7	68.7
France	118.9	126.2	125.0	146.4	181.9	234.3	255.2
GFR	883.2	833.7	807.1	901.9	1183.1	1505.6	1524.2
Eire	4.8	3.5	3.4	5.3	8.2	11.9	11.4
Italy	126.8	131.0	139.6	196.8	217.0	274.5	308.8
Netherlands	98.4	83.2	89.0	109.6	130.6	172.9	170.5
Spain	37.0	34.4	34.7	34.1	47.7	51.4	47.8
UK	134.1	113.8	114.3	144.9	175.3	208.2	269.2
Greece	42.9	21.6	24.3	36.8	33.9	43.5	52.2
Portugal	3.5	3.5	4.4	3.3	2.8	4.5	4.6
Σ EC	1545.6	1444.6	1433.0	1680.5	2129.1	2661.3	2813.0
Σ World	5141.6	4978.9	4867.1	5357.4	6106.2	6993.2	7862.0

(excluding USSR, Cuba, Nk, Alb, Mon, DDR, Bul)

Source : Direction of Trade Statistics Yearbook 1989 IMF

TABLE 5 : CMEA - EC TRADE
DDR 1982-1988

DDR   EXPORTS (from)   IMPORTS (to)

(m US $)

	EXPORTS (from)							IMPORTS (to)						
	1982	1983	1984	1985	1986	1987	1988	1982	1983	1984	1985	1986	1987	1988
Belgium-Lux	123.4	116.5	120.5	145.5	160.6	175.1	179.9	56.7	117.8	80.8	71.5	131.3	140.3	166.7
Denmark	145.7	156.8	164.0	164.3	166.7	143.5	137.6	33.9	42.0	36.6	38.4	52.9	71.4	124.4
France	258.4	250.5	236.0	266.2	354.6	372.7	415.4	283.8	283.8	233.0	229.7	371.2	421.9	385.1
GFR						3975.5	4060.4						4406.1	4326.5
Eire	8.4	6.6	9.2	9.5	14.6	11.5	12.0	5.1	3.7	3.0	2.7	3.3	5.8	14.0
Italy	147.7	108.2	103.8	115.2	171.7	179.9	192.7	138.1	93.4	144.2	114.8	210.1	257.3	289.6
Netherlands	195.0	210.2	142.9	187.8	184.9	179.8	179.1	111.5	111.5	97.2	102.4	146.1	254.9	292.5
Spain	85.1	103.1	75.2	45.7	61.9	55.2	67.8	63.6	46.2	66.0	116.0	73.9	41.9	93.5
UK	212.0	231.4	240.3	238.2	261.8	270.3	223.4	122.0	101.0	137.7	91.1	131.3	148.8	209.1
Greece	34.9	43.2	83.1	53.0	42.3	40.4	48.5	17.8	19.2	15.3	38.3	35.6	36.5	43.8
Portugal	11.7	18.6	19.6	21.8	16.2	18.4	13.3	6.1	3.3	5.8	4.3	3.7	5.5	5.4
Σ EC	*1222.3	*1244.6	*1194.3	*1247.2	*1435.3	5422.3	5530.1	*838.6	*821.9	*819.6	*809.2	*1159.5	5790.4	5950.6
Σ World	*5067.3	*5195.7	*4886.6	*4939.3	*5420.7	9862.4	10542.3	*4659.2	*5032.5	*4822.3	*4419.4	*5262.6	10938.5	11386.9

(excluding Cuba, Mon, Nk, Alb, USSR, Bul)

* Excluding GDR - FDR trade

Source : Direction of Trade Statistics Yearbook 1989 IMF

TABLE 6 : CMEA - EC TRADE
HUNGARY 1982-1988

HUNGARY   EXPORTS (from)   IMPORTS (to)

(m US $)

	EXPORTS (from)							IMPORTS (to)						
	1982	1983	1984	1985	1986	1987	1988	1982	1983	1984	1985	1986	1987	1988
Belgium-Lux	40.6	33.7	38.8	32.6	61.1	67.8	80.7	88.4	88.9	76.7	88.3	120.9	148.4	138.0
Denmark	32.0	32.2	32.6	32.5	39.1	41.3	50.8	35.6	30.7	28.7	35.6	36.9	46.0	49.7
France	132.3	134.0	142.7	115.0	142.1	180.0	201.4	195.7	159.5	139.7	151.6	177.8	189.8	185.1
GFR	673.3	644.4	638.6	680.5	770.5	938.6	1085.1	985.8	867.2	863.9	944.1	1188.9	1368.1	1293.8
Eire	4.0	3.0	4.0	4.0	6.0	6.0	5.0	4.0	7.0	7.0	8.0	12.0	14.0	15.0
Italy	302.5	289.5	281.2	251.2	292.5	345.0	419.2	240.4	196.7	195.8	230.3	260.5	263.8	295.9
Netherlands	91.5	84.1	94.0	78.2	103.5	103.0	117.2	120.5	106.0	103.4	107.3	136.3	146.1	165.4
Spain	9.2	11.5	14.4	12.0	16.4	24.6	32.1	32.2	27.5	41.4	41.9	48.4	35.8	35.7
UK	78.2	95.8	128.1	123.6	121.4	144.2	187.1	178.4	180.9	146.2	157.7	171.4	169.4	169.7
Greece	52.2	40.3	37.6	42.7	39.8	52.0	62.8	20.1	39.1	33.5	19.3	18.0	27.0	16.0
Portugal	2.3	1.7	1.5	1.9	2.7	4.3	4.4	4.0	3.4	4.0	3.9	4.2	8.5	7.4
Σ EC	1382.1	1370.2	1413.5	1374.2	1595.1	1906.8	2245.8	1905.1	1706.9	1640.3	1788.0	2175.3	2417.9	2371.7
Σ World	8779.3	8706.4	8568.3	8544.0	9174.1	9565.9	9956.1	8827.3	8519.3	8102.4	8235.6	9614.9	9864.0	9360.8

Source : Direction of Trade Statistics Yearbook 1989 IMF

44

TABLE 7 : CMEA - EC TRADE
POLAND 1982-1988

POLAND

(m US $)

	EXPORTS (from)							IMPORTS (to)						
	1982	1983	1984	1985	1986	1987	1988	1982	1983	1984	1985	1986	1987	1988
Belgium-Lux	113.0	94.0	99.0	110.0	109.0	127.0	152.0	84.0	90.0	114.0	105.0	102.0	108.0	137.0
Denmark	99.0	94.0	157.0	157.0	163.0	195.0	217.0	38.0	26.0	39.0	85.0	97.0	86.0	112.0
France	307.0	288.0	292.0	274.0	266.0	321.0	340.0	412.0	215.0	199.0	203.0	241.0	275.0	318.0
GFR	956.0	1007.0	1042.0	963.0	1092.0	1260.0	1506.0	734.0	720.0	784.0	972.0	1137.0	1341.0	1643.0
Eire	35.0	48.0	51.0	62.0	70.0	69.0	72.0	3.0	5.0	10.0	9.0	15.0	22.0	18.0
Italy	293.0	270.0	281.0	279.0	293.0	356.0	407.0	165.0	182.0	196.0	248.0	249.0	312.0	377.0
Netherlands	150.0	199.0	191.0	188.0	166.0	215.0	267.0	122.0	150.0	173.0	173.0	196.0	203.0	271.0
Spain	123.0	105.0	115.0	92.0	55.0	95.0	75.0	21.0	30.0	28.0	37.0	33.0	34.0	52.0
UK	401.0	572.0	478.0	375.0	415.0	452.0	532.0	321.0	382.0	386.0	236.0	268.0	297.0	313.0
Greece	56.0	52.0	42.0	14.0	23.0	40.0	48.0	12.0	10.0	16.0	12.0	7.0	18.0	22.0
Portugal	6.6	4.7	7.8	16.5	13.0	7.7	9.5	3.6	3.7	1.6	2.4	3.7	3.8	3.0
Σ EC	2539.6	2733.7	2755.8	2530.5	2665.0	3137.7	3625.5	1905.6	1813.7	1946.6	2082.4	2348.7	2699.8	3266.0
Σ World	11219.6	11576.7	11757.8	11505.5	12087.0	12212.7	13968.6	10254.6	10525.7	10584.6	11412.4	11105.4	10797.8	12154.0

Source : Direction of Trade Statistics Yearbook 1989 IMF

45

TABLE 8 : CMEA - EC TRADE
ROMANIA 1982-1988

ROMANIA

(m US $)

EXPORTS (from)

	1982	1983	1984	1985	1986	1987	1988
Belgium-Lux	99.0	49.0	60.0	46.0	45.0	53.0	53.0
Denmark	11.0	15.0	21.0	35.0	28.0	14.0	15.0
France	314.0	321.0	301.0	289.0	478.0	492.0	427.0
GFR	804.0	629.0	755.0	842.0	695.0	724.0	718.0
Eire	1.0	1.0	3.0	3.0	26.0	26.0	6.0
Italy	347.0	619.0	935.0	838.0	567.0	796.0	747.0
Netherlands	179.0	207.0	251.0	201.0	122.0	101.0	122.0
Spain	55.0	65.0	36.0	37.0	54.0	60.0	96.0
UK	193.0	275.0	240.0	302.0	116.0	137.0	163.0
Greece	221.0	292.0	188.0	109.0	49.0	62.0	75.0
Portugal	10.0	5.0	3.0	2.0	4.0	8.0	12.0
Σ EC	2185.0	2477.0	2793.0	2705.0	2185.0	2473.0	2435.0
Σ World	10123.0	10090.0	10720.0	11218.0	10792.0	12322.0	13953.0

IMPORTS (to)

	1982	1983	1984	1985	1986	1987	1988
Belgium-Lux	64.0	30.0	43.0	54.0	46.0	34.0	27.0
Denmark	5.0	3.0	5.0	6.0	10.0	6.0	5.0
France	141.0	105.0	125.0	116.0	156.0	116.0	119.0
GFR	405.0	268.0	305.0	294.0	342.0	327.0	327.0
Eire	3.0	1.0	1.0	1.0	3.0	1.0	
Italy	136.0	93.0	101.0	146.0	154.0	78.0	72.0
Netherlands	77.0	61.0	70.0	44.0	46.0	44.0	43.0
Spain	33.0	15.0	20.0	15.0	29.0	5.0	2.0
UK	223.0	124.0	160.0	157.0	120.0	92.0	89.0
Greece	77.0	49.0	39.0	43.0	47.0	47.0	57.0
Portugal	11.0	10.0	9.0	8.0	9.0	5.0	5.0
Σ EC	1175.0	760.0	878.0	885.0	962.0	756.0	747.0
Σ World	8323.0	7551.0	7557.0	8655.0	7681.0	8293.0	9285.0

Source : Direction of Trade Statistics Yearbook 1989 IMF

TABLE 9 : ROAD IMPORTS & EXPORTS. CMEA 1980, 1985 & 1986

By Road	Goods Entered (000T)			Goods Left (000T)			Transit (000T)		
	1980	1985	1986	1980	1985	1986	1980	1985	1986
BL	-	-	-	-	-	-	-	-	-
CZ	902	692	741	1369	1546	1556	-	-	-
DDR	608	920	1021	1615	2500	2573	132	408	425
H	434	1031	1153	871	1961	2138	743	2243	2423
PL	363	610	294	513	1098	668	753	895	773
ROM	-	-	-	-	-	-	-	-	-

Source : United Nations

47

Individual patterns of trade between EC member countries of Eastern Europe are not analysed here, and are left to the reader to dissect and amass from other sources such as the UN and IMF. For the moment, we shall turn to the individual road haulage markets of the CMEA in Europe and attempt to place their development, organisation, significance and role in perspective, in the next chapter.

4 The eastern bloc road haulage markets

Introduction

This section attempts to set out the reasons why the European Community and West European haulage operators might be interested in the activities of the East European haulage market both before and after the recent political and economic changes that have begun to take place. It goes on briefly, to examine the markets in each of the six countries concerned (Bulgaria, Czechoslovakia, DDR, Hungary, Poland and Romania) and explains why the report has concentrated only on four of them in any detail. Finally, it will act as an introduction to the case studies presented in the following Chapters 5 to 8.

Previous Work on East-West International Haulage

The main research previously published on the role of the European Community road hauliers in East-West European trade was that produced by the Economic and Social Committee of the European Communities (ESCEC, 1977). Although covering inland waterway and shipping as well, a major part of this report looked at the road haulage market of Eastern Europe, and, at that time, the steadily growing competition that was emerging. The report recognised this growth and the freedom given to Eastern Bloc hauliers in the West, to operate and acquire loads, compared to that for Western hauliers in the East. The ESCEC compiled the report to draw attention to this disparity and the effects it was having and would continue to have on transport operators in Western Europe.

In terms of road haulage operations, it produced a number of conclusions relevant to this research:

(i)   In the Eastern Bloc's (then) centrally controlled economies, foreign trade and international goods transport were in the hands of State monopolies. By comparison, most firms involved in road haulage in the west, were organised on a decentralised basis and formed part of the private sector. This general difference in organisation places western transport operators at a competitive disadvantage. Operating at their own risk in line with the principles of private enterprise, they must cover their full costs with the rates obtainable on the market, whereas the monopolies of the State trading countries apply completely different principles when determining their costs and risks and fixing their rates.

(ii)   The running of international transport operations in State trading countries had to fit in with national economic plans. The aim was to give the State the power to control transport and capacity which it could use to attain the targets set in national plans and which it can exercise in the fields of international trade and traffic too. The Eastern Bloc countries do this by selling exports CIF, and purchasing imports FOB. As a result, they retain full control over the carriage of their imports and exports since, as the players of the freight, they are free to choose the carrier.

The result was identified in road haulage, as a strong- hold by East European hauliers over East-West and West-East transport, caused by the conditions of competition being unevenly balanced, and leading to the sustained expansion of Eastern Bloc Hauliers in bilateral traffic between CMEA and EC countries.

The ESCEC suggested a number of general 'actions' which would improve the situation, and then a number of 'actions' specific to the international road haulage market.

General actions (applicable to all transport modes) included the following.

"It is necessary to work towards the following common targets in international traffic between Community and East-European State-trading countries:

Community land and sea transport operators should have a fair share of East-West traffic, due regard being paid to the special structure and conditions of transport in the Member States. The purpose of efforts here must be to prevent the CMEA countries from reaping all the benefits and to work towards effective and - at all events - evenly matched reciprocity. It would appear advisable to do something about the cif and fob clauses in supply contracts so as to ensure equal access to the market.

Workers employed by Community operators should be ensured legal and social protection when in Eastern Bloc countries.

Consideration should be given to the social aspects of the problems posed in East-West transport by unfair competition and especially to the employment question and the reper- cussions on other sectors of the economy.

The administrative formalities in international transport - and especially at frontiers - should be simplified and aligned.

The special taxes and discriminatory charges in CMEA countries should be abolished.

The transport activities of CMEA countries should be monitored in order to guarantee reciprocity with regard to the right of establishment, the acquisition of holdings and the access to cargoes/loads.

International Road Haulage Actions

The following are the main measures to give Western road hauliers an equal share of traffic between Member States and Eastern Bloc countries:

Agreements on equal access to the market through a system of licences for bilateral and transit traffic.

Agreements on access to loads through ensuring the freedom of establishment coupled with possibilities for securing cargoes (if need be, traffic sharing agreements could be concluded).

Ban on exorbitant road tolls and transit levies.

Rules governing the picking up of return loads or additional loads in transit.

Reduction in the high visa fees charged by CMEA countries and introduction of permanent visas for lorry crews.

Recognition of the green insurance card by all CMEA countries, thus putting an end to the need for separate insurances to be taken out for vehicles.

Simplification and acceleration of customs procedures.

Guarantee of adequate stop-overs for lorry crews.

Legal protection for lorry crews involved in accidents.

The Committee noted that Eastern Bloc operators have established permanent agencies in neighbouring Western countries, whereas Western carriers and forwarding agents are not able to set up such establishments in CMEA countries. Eastern Bloc operators can thus not only compete freely for cargoes, but also keep a direct eye on developments on the different markets; full use is also made of the business opportunities they find. This gives Eastern Bloc operators a major competitive advantage.

In view of this situation and the fact that

(a)   it is difficult for Western firms to set up branches in CMEA countries,

(b)   even if they do succeed, these branches are restricted in their freedom of movement and

(c)   genuine reciprocity is therefore unattainable,

the establishment by CMEA countries in the Community of agencies or firms coming under their control, should be supervised.

This restriction or ban should include firms which are controlled directly or indirectly by natural or legal persons from a CMEA country or by such a country itself. Control here means the influencing of the firm's decisions with regard, in particular, to the use of transport means or market strategy.

Finally, freedom of establishment in CMEA countries would have to be backed up by appropriate freedom to secure cargoes in these countries and by improved access to cargoes before it could be said that Western carriers were given the same treatment as their Eastern Bloc counterparts".

In some more detail, the ESCEC report noted the following characteristics and problems of the East-West International road haulage market before going on to make some recommendations about how to improve the situation from the point of view of EC hauliers. This section is taken largely from the ESCEC report.

"Road haulage to and from the Eastern Bloc countries shows a similar pattern to that observed in other modes of transport but international road haulage differs from sea transport in being closely regulated and from rail transport in that one and the same firm carries the goods throughout the journey.

The Eastern Bloc countries are thus able to keep traffic under very close surveillance. Because their foreign trade agencies try to obtain control over the carriage of goods at the time of the negotiations of the contract or by applying specific pressures, the bilateral agreements between them and Western European countries designed to ensure that each gets its fair share of traffic, are relatively or completely ineffective.

Although still a relatively small part of the total, the volume of EEC-Eastern Europe traffic carried by road has in recent years been increasing at a faster than average rate.

In the case of France, the proportion is seldom more than 20% (GDR), and with several trading partners (Yugoslavia, Czechoslovakia, Hungary and Bulgaria) it lies between 10 and 20%. In traffic to and from the USSR it is under 1%. With Poland and Romania, road haulage's share of traffic is under 3%, owing to the importance of sea transport in trade with these countries.

The proportion of traffic carried by road in West Germany's total trade with Eastern Europe is 7% and it is noteworthy that the statistics of the German authorities show a 100% increase in lorry movements in trade with Eastern Europe (including Yugoslavia) between 1970 (62,100 entries and exits) and 1975 (125,000).

Statistics published by the French Customs also show an increase in the tonnage transported by road to and from Eastern Europe over the same period, both in absolute terms and as a proportion of the total traffic volume. This situation reflects an increase in general goods traffic and in "turnkey" construction work, for both of which road transport is the ideal medium. It also indicates the importance Eastern Bloc countries attach to developing their road haulage industries.

The development of trade with Eastern countries obviously depends on decisions taken in the five-year plans, which show these countries' efforts to correct the current imbalance in their foreign trade. In this context, there may be a greater flow to the West of finished goods manufactured with the help of Western capital in Eastern countries. A more balanced pattern of trade, particularly as regards finished goods, should also lead to a better balance in the transport of goods best suited to carriage by road.

The distribution of traffic between national operators was examined with the use of examples from France, West Germany, Denmark and the Benelux countries.

The share of French hauliers in trade with Yugoslavia, USSR and Romania is around 30%. They have more than 30% of traffic with the GDR, Poland and Hungary, and less than 30% of that with Czechoslovakia and Bulgaria. Only 13% of imports from the last two countries are moved by French carriers. In the case of the USSR, the only return loads are goods for exhibitions and trade fairs.

In the case of traffic in which Western Germany is involved, EEC hauliers' share of transport to and from Romania and Hungary is about 15%. In traffic with Czechoslovakia and Poland the proportion is higher (around 40%), while with Bulgaria and USSR it is under 10%.

In the case of Denmark, the proportion is almost nil in traffic with the GDR and Romania, 5% in that with USSR, 15% in that with Czechoslovakia and between 30 and 50% in traffic with Hungary and Poland. The pattern is the same in traffic involving the Benelux countries, except that USSR traffic is even more lopsided. Over a two-year period, Belgian lorries made only three trips to Russia.

The East Europeans are also taking an increasing share of third-country traffic between the EEC and the Middle East, in which Bulgaria is particularly involved. Thanks to its geographical location, it can carry goods to and from the Middle East and West Europe, in transit through its own territory. This also allows it to obtain preferential tax treatment for transit traffic through Yugoslavia and Turkey. For these various reasons, Bulgaria is building up its lorry fleets and making efforts to penetrate not only third-country traffic to the Middle East but also all intra-European and even African traffic. In 1973, West German third-country traffic represented 15.3% of all Bulgarian-carried traffic originating in West Germany; this had shot up to 57.1% by 1974 and to 86.9% by 1975.

In road transport, as in the other modes, the East European State-run undertakings make their foreign suppliers and customers sell fob or "ex-works" and buy cif or delivered to destination. In this way they bring carriage of the goods under their control, and impose their own forwarding agents, or agents acting for them in the EEC, and their own haulage contractors on Western exporters and importers.

The progressive abandonment of the road transport of goods to the East European buyers has led, according to the French Foreign Trade Centre, to the carriage being taken completely out of the consignor's control. Before being paid, the exporter generally has to produce a certificate from the mandatory agent to the effect that the latter has taken charge of the consignment. This generally results in a monopoly situation which is reflected in higher transport costs. For example, when the selling price is stipulated "free frontier", the charge made by the mandatory agent for carriage from factory to frontier is often exorbitant, and in specific instances has been found to cover carriage to the destination.

With EEC firms excluded from the handling of consignments, users also face excessive commission, packing and storage charges. Investigations carried out particularly by German chambers of commerce and the French Foreign Trade Centre have shown the drawbacks suffered by exporters and importers, whatever the form of transport used. In the case of road transport the difficulties are made more serious by the fact that the goods exported from the EEC are generally better suited to road transport than the goods imported. Thus, the loss of control over the carriage of his goods handicaps the exporter in carrying out his export contract.

The forwarding agents put loads first and foremost on Eastern Bloc lorries, except when the quota has been used up. In that case they give the loads to EEC operators either as far as the frontier, where they are reloaded on to other lorries, or right to the destination. But the EEC operators are only acting here as sub-contractors, and have no hope of finding a return load at their destination. It has proved impossible (except in one known case between French and Hungarian operators) to establish co-operation for the purposes of obtaining return loads in the foreign country, as is common practice between operators in the Community.

In CMEA countries the foreign trade agencies have sole authority for road transport. They ignore bids by EEC operators, and other bodies, such as ministries of transport and road haulage associations, refuse to intervene. The case of EEC lorries obtaining loads in Eastern Europe concern purchases "ex-works" by Community importers who bear the cost of carriage. EEC lorry operators cannot be paid in convertible currency by Eastern Bloc consignors.

The social aspect of the situation as regards competition in East-West transport arises principally in relation to employment.

As a result of the increased activity of the East Europeans in this market, several thousand East European lorries now travel to and from EEC countries. Further market penetration by East European

State-run undertakings therefore has disquieting implications for employment in the Community.

The social protection obtained by trade organisations under collective agreements must be backed up by vigilance on the part of the governments to prevent a recurrence of abnormal incidents (eg problems relating to accident insurance, medical care and attention, social insurance matters, imprisonment of drivers without trial, etc.)

The report of the ESCEC went on to comment on a number of other relevant issues - including that of bilateral agreements. Bilateral licensing procedures have already been laid down in administrative agreements at Government level.

International road transport between EEC Member States and Eastern Bloc countries is - in all but a few cases - governed by bilateral agreements. These agreements follow the same pattern as other agreements concluded between European States. They stipulate in each case that the Governments of the two signatory States are to grant an equal number of licences to carriers from each State, giving access to the other signatory State's territory. As a general rule, these licences cover bilateral transport operations and transit journeys undertaken by freight and passenger transport vehicles. The carriage of goods is authorised on both the outward and return legs of bilateral services.

The bilateral agreements concluded between some West European States allow a vehicle on its homeward journey to carry between a State through which it passes in transit and the State in which it is registered.

Thus, a French vehicle returning home from Eastern Europe can carry between the Federal Republic of Germany and France. On the other hand, the same vehicle is forbidden to carry on its outward journey between the Federal Republic of Germany and an Eastern Bloc country. Similarly, the vehicle is forbidden to operate between an Eastern Bloc country and the Federal Republic.

Third-country transport operations, ie between two States other than that in which the vehicle is registered, are, in principle, banned. for example, a vehicle from a West European State cannot carry between the East European State which is the vehicle's destination on its outward journey, and a Central European State.

However, such journeys are permitted by way of exception when the vehicle passes in transit through the country in which it is registered. Thus, Polish, Hungarian, Czechoslovakian, Romanian or Yugoslavian carriers can carry between EEC Member States and the USSR when the bilateral agreements allow them to. French or German transport operators can pick up goods in Spain for carriage to Eastern Europe, and Benelux operators can undertake similar hauls from Britain. Similarly, goods can be carried between the EEC and the Middle East by undertakings from the Eastern European States which lie on the route.

Because of the commercial policy of their governments described above, East European carriers are often able to take up quotas more fully than their EEC counterparts. Once these quotas have been exhausted, the East European may sometimes put their loads on Western lorries.

However, it has been found that by using semi-trailers drawn by tractor units from a country on the route it is possible to get round the quota. For instance, Russian semi-trailers coupled to Belgian tractor units have managed to get into Holland after the quota had been reached. The same type of operation is planned with German tractor units hauling Bulgarian semi-trailers.

Some governments are clamping down on articulated vehicles made up of units of different nationalities, and are requiring a permit for the trailer unit if it is from a different country than the tractor unit.

In addition, transport operators from some countries belonging to the European Conference of Ministers of Transport are able to operate freely between these countries under the terms of multilateral authorizations. These operators occasionally provide tractor units for Eastern Bloc countries, whose vehicles thus find easier access to the countries of the ECMT and the EEC.

Whatever the nationality of the carrier, carriage is on the whole in the hands of the official agents of the socialist countries (USSR, Poland, GDR, Czechoslovakia, Hungary, Bulgaria), acting directly or indirectly in the West. The big Eastern Bloc agencies have set up branches in West Germany, Belgium and the Netherlands. In countries where their establishment is restricted by the government (eg. in France, only Poland has an official agency), the East European official agencies have Western agents acting for them.

The activities of these Western agents are still preferable to those of the direct representatives of the State agencies, though it does not alter the situation much. The key factor in this worrying trend for the Community transport industry is the abandonment of control over the carriage of their goods by EEC exporters and importers.

This commercial network in the West means that the agents of the State-run organizations in Eastern Bloc countries know immediately when contracts are concluded. The agents then approach the Community firm involved in the transaction and if necessary quote an uneconomic rate when there is any danger of competition.

Practices amounting to cut-throat competition are also used to penetrate third-country traffic, to which the transport undertakings of some Eastern Bloc states are increasingly turning their attention. EEC agents now have no hesitation in doing business with Eastern Bloc transport undertakings in this traffic in which tax discrimination destroys any semblance of healthy competition.

The ESCEC ascertained that, in the field of cross-frontier goods traffic, the principle of reciprocity determines the basic objectives and tasks first and foremost. The EEC transport industry demands a greater share than at present of East-West transport. In making this demand, it subscribes to the principles of free choice of carrier, non-discrimination and apportionment of work on the basis of uniform conditions of competition. Experience in the field of transport integration in Europe also shows that the principle of reciprocity has also helped to reduce tensions and prevent conflicts. These principles should also be borne in mind in the development of road transport with Eastern Europe.

Measures dealing with access to the market and to loads will have to be adopted in the main if Western road hauliers are to be given an equal share of cross-frontier traffic to and from Eastern Bloc countries. Both the Community and the individual Member States could resort to compulsory licensing for foreign vehicles engaged in inter-state and transit traffic.

The Section has noted that the provisions of the bilateral agreements with the Eastern Bloc countries, which were concluded on the same basis as the bilateral agreements between Member States of the European Economic Community or the European Conference of Ministers of Transport, are applied under very special economic and commercial conditions. This leads to lopsidedness in the two parties' shares of traffic and to an increasing monopoly of the Eastern Bloc countries State trade agencies because of the control they have over the carriage of goods.

Therefore, the Section calls upon the political authorities to take steps to correct the present unfavourable and dangerous situation regarding competition in this sector.

The ESCEC felt that the Community had a twofold mission. Firstly, it must encourage coherent action for the promotion of EEC transport, and, secondly, it must co-ordinate the specific measures taken by Member States.

The establishment of a balance in road haulage must, therefore, be one of the aims of the Community's policy on trade relations with Eastern Europe. The idea of reciprocity, which was also mentioned in the Final Act of the Helsinki agreements, now remains to be put into practice.

There must be a balance in transport services to prevent monopolies from emerging and impairing the competitiveness of the EEC's economy in the long run. Accordingly, loads must be shared out equitably between each international trading partner's carriers. The Community authorities must ensure that on both the import and export markets, EEC carriers can operate under commercial, technical social and legal conditions comparable to those on other international transport markets.

The Commission is able to intervene and align specific aspects of Member States' transport policies by encouraging the Member States to take co-ordinated action on problems posed by traffic to and from Eastern Bloc countries. This co-ordinated action could embrace the alignment of rules on bilateral traffic through the introduction of transport licences in all Member States.

Joint action should be planned to deal with transit traffic, which poses special problems for the EEC countries travelled through. These countries could be given a share of certain traffic flows, especially in the case of stock- reduction measures under the CAP which usually involve EEC financial assistance. This joint action could also cover transport operations to Member States which could be carried out by vehicles returning from Eastern Europe and not passing in transit through their country of registration.

This joint action might also enable a common position to be reached on restrictions on traffic. These restrictions are particularly severe in the Soviet Union, where many roads are out of bounds for foreign vehicles. As a result vehicles have to travel further to reach their destinations, and Soviet territory cannot be crossed by EEC vehicles en route to the Middle East.

In addition, visa formalities (especially in the USSR) and transit taxes (as in Poland) are barriers which slow journeys down and make them more expensive. The Community must take stock of these various difficulties and raise them in the negotiations it conducts as an entity with Eastern Bloc countries.

Should political difficulties arise on account of the nature of relations between the EEC and Eastern Bloc countries or the organisation of the latter within CMEA, the Member States will continue to bear full responsibility for the organisation of transport with Eastern Bloc countries.

A particular medium for such action would be bilateral road transport agreements with these countries. These agreements must give the public authorities the power to ensure a greater share of transport for EEC operators on the basis of reciprocity through the threat of retaliatory action.

Furthermore, the scope of these licences should be restricted and permission to put loads on East European vehicles in EEC countries should be made conditional on reciprocal treatment being accorded in Eastern Bloc countries to EEC hauliers.

It has been seen how quotas can be circumvented by using semitrailers hauled by EEC tractor units. The French Government has now introduced for Eastern Bloc countries a system of permits based on the country of registration of the semitrailer. This method should be adopted by all Member States for this type of traffic if effective control is to be exercised over the activities of Eastern Bloc operators.

Eastern European operators are of course also making efforts to penetrate transport between the EEC and third countries. Here, too, the exemptions for triangular traffic should be restricted, or indeed suspended altogether, if reciprocity is not effectively granted for traffic originating in East European countries.

Reciprocity must include payment of EEC hauliers in convertible currencies by the consignors in Eastern Europe and abolition of the de facto monopoly of East European State forwarding agents and the agents acting for them in the West".

Despite the exhortations presented within the ESCEC report, very little if anything was achieved in redressing the imbalance of trade carryings between East and West, and vice versa from 1977 to 1989. The Commission of the European Communities has continued to monitor the patterns of haulier nationality in East-West traffic since the ESCEC Report of 1977, and has published comparative data for 1981, 1984 and 1987. This data, although limited by the statistical unreliability and also the absence of information from the East, has shown that the disparity in carryings between Western and Eastern hauliers has grown - despite the existence of bilateral agreements aimed at sharing the trade, because the West's share is rarely used up, whereas that of the East very frequently is. To quote the 1987 Report (Commission of the European Communities; 1989):

"Supposing that the EC-Eastern Bloc companies have an equal share of the cross-trade, the market shares of the two blocs in total East-West traffic were:

        1981 - 41% (EC) and 59% (East Bloc)

        1984 - 45% (EC) and 55% (East Bloc)

        1985 - 44% (EC) and 56% (East Bloc)

        1986 - 41% (EC) and 59% (East Bloc)

The flow to and from the DDR being approximately 40% of the total, dominates the East-West traffic substantially. Therefore, it can be useful to look at the East-West traffic minus the relation with the DDR. In that case, the position of the Member State hauliers is even more unfavourable:

        1985 - 43% (EC) & 57% (East Bloc)

1986 - 39% (EC) & 61% (East Bloc)

In rather more detail, the Commission also presented the shares in tonnes transported by hauliers of Member States and those of the CMEA countries, as a percentage of the bilateral total for 1986. The balance, where needed, represents cross traders.

A clear dominance in favour of the Eastern Bloc in almost all trades is apparent, but note the exceptions of Denmark, where full data is available, and Spain and Portugal, where the amount of traffic is too low to make statistical analysis unreliable.

During 1989, the first major economic and political changes in Eastern Europe changed many of the concerns and attitudes towards the European Community - including the trucking industry which over the last year or so has come to be viewed as more in need of help - advice, than in need of defence. However, one should not overlook the fact that many of the unfair trading practices identified in East European trucking prior to the 1989/1990 political and economic changes, still exist and remain as relevant today as ever. For example:

(i)   there remain quite extensive indirect subsidies of East European hauliers, including some international operations;

(ii)   there remains the widespread belief that the state will continue to bail out bankrupt trucking industries when state owned, and despite modern bankruptcy plans;

(iii)   hard currency remains a central issue and will encourage State hauliers to continue to trade at lower than cost to attract hard currency payments and reduce hard currency outgoings;

(iv)   there remain almost non-existent tax and insurance regimes, and the opportunity to purchase East European maufactured trucks, subsidised in production.

Consequently, even though it is thirteen years since the ESCEC report identified these and many other issues, this research indicates these issues as still very relevant to the problem of international haulage between East and West Europe. However, the new regime that has developed

SHARE OF TRAFFIC BY STATE (%) 1986

	SU	PL	DDR	CZ	H	BG	RO	AVERAGE
D	3-91	50-41	47-53	43-56	17-65	8-86	27-65	27.9-65.3
F	14-74	20-64	24-61	10-75	10-66	0-94	16-68	13.0-71.7
I	44-56	71-29	49-51	39-61	41-59	30-70	58-42	47.4-52.6
NL	15-83	48-38	24-60	19-69	27-56	15-78	46-40	27.7-60.6
B	1-94	28-48	12-65	4-82	18-54	8-85	9-75	11.4-71.9
L	0-100	0-90	0-92	0-62	0-85	0-100	0-73	0-86.0
GB	44-18	10-88	4-33	5-92	6-90	58-27	28-60	22.1-58.3
IRL	0	0	36-0	7-94	0-100	0	0	14.3-64.7
DK	47-0	77-15	32-32	43-40	49-37	3-56	90-3	48.7-26.1
GR	1-99	23-73	33-49	38-60	35-64	66-34	50-49	35.1-61.1
E	0-68	94-3	50-20	51-37	0	0	0	48.8-32.0
P	0	4-61	24-0	0-78	0	0	0	9.3-46.3
AVERAGE	16.9-68.3	38.6-50.0	27.8-43.0	21.6-67.2	20.3-67.6	20.9-70.0	36.0-52.8	

Source : Commission of the European Communities

throughout Eastern Europe in varying forms and to varying degrees, does pose a number of new questions that need to be addressed including in particular:

(i)   What help is needed to revitalise trucking within the Eastern European countries as part of the broader attempt to rebuild the Eastern Bloc economies?

(ii)   In what ways can the international trucking sector be made more efficient, and how can it combine the real needs of hard currency earnings, with true commercial practise and realistic pricing? What needs are there for technical developments, new investment, restructuring, management training, economic aid and more?

This report goes on to examine these questions in the light of recent developments and the problems associated with continued unfair trading practices.

However, before we do that, first a few brief words about the countries and companies chosen for case study appraisal. Although this research was concerned with all six of the CMEA East European hauliers, whilst excluding the Soviet Union, Yugoslavia and Albania as explained earlier, in fact only four were covered in any real detail. The four chosen were Bulgaria, Czechoslovakia, Hungary and Poland, with the two which have been largely neglected being the German Democratic Republic (DDR), and Romania. There were a number of positive reasons behind this choice:

(i)   Changes occurring in the DDR, in particular, the rapid progress towards reunification of East and West Germany made study of the international road haulage sector very difficult in circumstances which would have produced few meaningful results.

(ii)   The Hungarian, Polish and Bulgarian fleets were identified as the most progressive and most significant operators in and from Eastern Europe and those whose impact was likely to be notable in future in East-West transport and in the context of the Single European Market.

(iii)   Romania, like the DDR, but for different reasons and in a differing way, was a very difficult market to study. A visit in pre- revolution days in 1989, despite official approval and considerable courtesy and politeness, produced very little information at all. Romtrans, the international haulier, was presented as an efficient, go-ahead, independent concern, free to act commercially and largely unsubsidised using the most modern of equipment and operating in a Romanian market freely open to Western hauliers. In practice, the opposite was clearly the case as the company operated only Romanian made trucks, of great age, low reliability and poor quality; it was highly subsidised and operated as an arm of the State; it was totally uncommercial in its practices, and run as a combination of a hard-currency earner and a means to further defence and other related ambitions; and its market was almost totally closed to western hauliers.

No details were forthcoming from any source and hence it was impossible to reach any meaningful conclusions - a situation compounded by the political changes of 1989 and 1990, which have plunged the company into even more chaos.

Clearly Romtrans is an insignificant player in the international haulage market, and unlikely to be of any great interest in the short term at least, to the European Community and western hauliers. The main concern will be in determining how the west can aid Romtrans and the haulage market of Romania in the future, in the process of redeveloping the country as a whole. Certainly, considerable quantities of technical and management training and the like will be needed.

(iv)   The Bulgarian, Czechoslovakian, Hungarian and Polish international haulage operators were very willing to co-operate and discuss their daily operations, planning and policies for their companies, and to discuss the future in the new economic and political climate. This made analysis considerably easier.

Hence, the four case studies of international truck operations that follow cover Bulgaria, Czechoslovakia, Hungary and Poland. In each the issues identified by the ESCEC in their report of 1977, and the challenges of the new era in commerce in the East, are considered. In the concluding chapter, some thoughts in relation to the impact of the Single European

Market on Eastern European hauliers, will be considered, and the main themes and needs of Eastern Europe in the haulage market will be analysed.

5 Bulgaria

Introduction

Bulgaria is a relatively small country in Eastern Europe with a population of nine million (1988), bordered by Romania, Yugoslavia, Greece and Turkey. It has direct access to the Black Sea through major ports at Bourgas and Varna.

As in the other Central and Eastern European countries, the process of political change has accelerated in Bulgaria in recent months. The resignation on 10 November 1989 of Todor Zhivkov, the country's leader for thirty five years, has brought to power a new generation which is sympathetic to the ideas of Gorbachev.

In January the National Assembly scrapped those Articles of the Constitution which refer to the leading role of the Communist Party. The thirteen opposition parties and social movements working together under the umbrella of the Union of Democratic Forces (UDF) opened a series of round table talks with the government to discuss the country's future. On 2 February the XIV Extraordinary Congress of the Communist Party adopted a resolution in favour of political pluralism and parliamentary democracy, without however abandoning its allegiance to Marxism.

A reformer, Andrei Lukanov, Minister for External Relations, since August 1989, was elected Prime Minister by parliament on 5 February. His attempt to form a government of national unity failed, and instead he formed a Communist government which has continued the policies of the previous government.

On 3 April Parliament elected Ptar Mladenov President. The House passed an amendment to the Constitution under which Bulgaria ceased to be a socialist republic, and adopted laws on the formation of political parties and electoral procedures. Elections were called for 10 and 17 June which resulted in the election of the Communists once more with a small majority.

The democratic process is overshadowed by the problem of the Moslem minority. Tensions between ethnic groups came to a head in 1984 with a campaign to "Bulgarianise" Turkish names and a series of discriminatory measures against the Turkish language and Moslem customs and practices. The restrictions were lifted by the new government in December 1989. Despite opposition from the non-Turkish majority, the government has largely succeeded in imposing its policy.

In recent years Bulgaria has become an industrialised country. National income increased more than fourteen- fold between 1965 and 1987. Bulgaria's Five Year Plan for 1986-1990, like that of the other Comecon countries, concentrated on scientific and technological development, energy production, the modernisation of plant and the re- organisation of the country's external trade.

Official growth figures (6.2% in 1988, compared with 5.1% in 1987) are over-optimistic as the figures have not been adjusted to take account of price rises caused by the decentralisation of management and the emphasis placed on technological development.

The industrial sector accounts for some 60% of the national income. Official figures indicate good results in the priority industrial sectors, with a gross rise in production of 18.1% in electronics, 8% in heavy machinery and 5% in the chemicals sector. Results were below average in the mining sector (+4.1%) and the agro-industrial sector (+3.3%).

The current restructuring in this sector is aimed at increasing production in the metallurgical and electronics industries.

Bulgaria produces less than one third of its energy needs. It is completely dependent on the Soviet Union for supplies of crude oil and gas, and has made the development of subsidiary sources of energy a priority. The country's first nuclear power station was built in 1974 by Soviet engineers, and in 1988 it accounted for 35.6% of total electricity generation. A second nuclear plant is currently under construction.

The transport sector has major financing problems. 88% of goods by volume are transported by road. Of 36,988km of road only 242km is of motorway standard. 40% of the railway network is electrified.

Production of consumer goods, although up in 1988, remains inadequate despite the fact that a quarter of total state investment is spent on its development. At the end of 1988 there were 480 state firms producing consumer goods; between 1989 and 1990 another 390 were expected to start production and 100 new small-scale private firms to be formed. The object of this is to provide jobs for workers made redundant in other sectors.

The "new economic mechanisms" introduced in agriculture in 1979 and in industry in 1982, and the "restructuring" of the economy announced by the National Assembly which has been underway since 1987 have not brought about major changes in the economic system. The changes introduced in 1987 and 1988 have been restricted to macroeconomic management, but have had little effect on microeconomics, the basis of entrepreneurial activity.

Few satisfactory results emerged from the reforms carried out in 1982 to improve firm's efficiency by closing down unprofitable enterprises, cutting subsidies and linking wages to production. Further reforms were introduced in 1986, 1987 and 1988 to re-organise firms on the basis of autonomy. Successive re-organisations coupled with a lack of coherent policies were the cause of considerable confusion. It was to solve this problem that Decree Law No 56 was adopted by the Council of State on 19 January 1989. This Decree, superseding previous legislation, for the first time allowed private firms to be set up with less than ten employees. The Decree states that "the firm is the basic productive unit of the State"; this represents progress on the road towards a mixed economy.

Nonetheless, a memorandum sent by the Bulgarian authorities to the Commission in its capacity as co- ordinator of the Group of 24 shows that they have opted for a gradualist approach, rather than radical economic reform. Direct state intervention in the management of firms will merely be "phased out".

The reform of the wholesale prices system is expected to be completed this year, with prices being brought more or less into line with the world market. (23% of prices were reformed in 1988, and the 1989 reform was to cover 65-70% of wholesale prices). However, prices of raw materials and certain consumer goods will remain controlled "for as long as necessary".

The "restructuring" of the economy is based on the setting up of two free zones, nine large economic regions (in place of the existing twenty eight) and eight commercial banks.

The main purpose of the free zones (covering the ports of Vidin and Ruse on the Danube) is to stimulate economic initiative in respect of trade and the supply of goods and services, for the purpose of accelerating the accumulation of foreign exchange. A number of firms from France, Italy, Germany, Belgium and the USA have made initial contacts, but the zones are not yet operational.

The banking system is being reorganised, and new commercial banks, are being set up in order to facilitate the establishment of new firms. The banks will provide loans for the new firms and liquidate unprofitable ones. The Central Bank of Bulgaria will be restricted to the normal functions of a central bank.

The introduction of a value added tax is being contemplated. Pending its introduction, an income tax system was being phased in. Corporation tax rebates would be granted only in cases where the tax exceeded 50%.

With regard to foreign investment, the Decree Law allows foreigners to "do business independently or via a subsidiary or joint venture in Bulgaria". A foreign shareholding in a Bulgarian company may not normally exceed 49%, except with government authorisation. There are at present 200 companies of this kind. A subsequent amendment was made to the Council's Decree Law, stipulating a 40% tax rate for foreign-owned firms and 30% for joint ventures, the lowest level in the CMEA.

Bulgaria has considerable agricultural potential which is at present under-exploited. The agricultural sector is in economic crisis and has recently been declared a priority area by the state. Agriculture accounts for 27% of GNP, the highest proportion in any Eastern European country.

Agriculture is almost entirely collectivised. The private sector, although confined to some 10% of total land area, provides about 25% of total production (particularly maize, meat, eggs and vegetables). 20% of the workforce is employed in agriculture but the agricultural population is ageing, often insufficient for the tasks required of it and poorly trained.

Agriculture is of the Mediterranean type. The main crops are cereals, fruit and vegetables (in particular tomatoes), tobacco, sunflowers, sugar beet, aromatic and medicinal plants and honey. Animal products (mainly from sheep and pigs) now account for the bulk of production (58% by value of total production in 1988). Sheep and cattle farming is mainly geared to milk production. Yields remain low and Bulgaria has been forced to tackle major cattle feed shortages by importing massive quantities of soya cake; this has pushed up the burden of external debt.

The agro-food trade balance is in surplus, except with the USA and West Germany. The EEC has an agro-food trade deficit with Bulgaria (FF 15m in 1988). Bulgaria's main customers are the CMEA countries, especially the USSR.

Bulgaria's main exports are: tobacco, wine, fresh and processed fruit and vegetables, sheep, meat and offal (especially poultry), honey and aromatic and medicinal plants. Imports are restricted by the shortage of foreign exchange. They consist mainly of essential goods such as cereals, maize, animal feed, citrus fruits, cocoa and sugar cane.

Although the country has considerable agricultural potential including fertile land and favourable climatic conditions, Bulgarian agriculture at present has many handicaps: lack of investment, inadequate inputs, obsolete and inadequate irrigation and drainage, old plants, insufficient storage capacity causing high wastage (approx 30% of the harvest), a decrepit transport system and archaic sales and distribution networks.

The Bulgarian Government recently adopted a number of measures to encourage private enterprise in agriculture: the lifting of restrictions on the farming of land, a free choice of methods of production and the opportunity to export directly. There is a trend towards more flexible structures. Investment is picking up, particularly in machinery for the agro-food industry. The Government has also decided to set up an agricultural credit bank, and to liberalise the prices of certain agricultural products (the State will however continue to control the price of bread, milk, meat, sugar, oil and baby foods).

For the time being, and for the third consecutive year, agricultural production continues to fall. State prices are felt to be too low and force producers to cut back production in order to avoid expenditure on equipment and fertilizers, the costs of which continue to rise steadily. The implementation of the land law which is favourable to private property could however radically change the situation of Bulgarian agriculture in view of the traditionally high output in the private sector and possible improvements in productivity and yields.

Trucking in Bulgaria

Trucking in Bulgaria, and in the international markets of Europe in particular, is a major industry and one of the Bulgarian State's more successful enterprises.

Domestic trucking is undertaken by sixty five local enterprises, which emerged from a single state enterprise. Together they operate about 120.000 vehicles. These relatively new local operations remain entirely state owned, but have been given a number of new economic and managerial freedoms to increase competitiveness and efficiency. One result of this has been that they now operate internationally, in competition with the established and highly successful international trucking company So-mat.

So-mat (basically 'Sofia Autotransport') was formed in 1960 specifically to operate internationally, as a branch of the domestic trucking industry, and since a state decree of 1975, has had to operate profitably as a hard currency earner.

Although it is difficult to be absolutely accurate, So-mat operates about 3,800 trucks in the international market. Accuracy is a problem simply because there are continual acquisitions and disposals of trucks from the fleet. The significant size of So-mat makes it the largest trucking company in the world.

73

Four types of vehicles are operated, all of Western manufacture:

- Mercedes-Benz   - 50% of the fleet
- Volvo   - 20% of the fleet
- Fiat/Iveco Ford   - 18% of the fleet
- Renault   - 12% of the fleet

No East European manufactured trucks are owned or operated for good marketing, economic and service quality reasons.

So-mat is almost exclusively an international operation, although under Bulgarian law it has full rights to operate domestically if it so wishes. These rights are exercised occasionally when capacity allows and when demand is low for international services. The number of trucks in domestic service at any one time is about a hundred. It is a market that provides only local currency at domestic rates and hence is unprofitable, particularly since costs remain those dictated by operating expensive Western made trucks.

All So-mat's trucks are purchased for cash from hard currency earnings. None are now purchased by the state, from state revenue. Average age of the fleet is difficult to estimate, but about 50% is over five years old, and the remainder, under. A small proportion of the fleet (some 2-4%) is over twelve years old.

Investment in new trucks is made about every three years when bulk purchases are made from single manufacturers to achieve discounts and economies of scale. Each purchase is about 200-300 trucks in size.

Four different makes are retained to increase diversity and ensure bargaining power at the purchase stage. Each truck type is known to have its own advantages and disadvantages and, therefore, there is little sense in concentrating upon only one make.

So-mat has six operational branches in the company, overseen by a central head office. Each branch is part of the main group and not separated financially, organis- ationally or in any other way. Hence collaboration, rather than competition is the order of the day.

Each branch operates a single depot which concentrates on a single vehicle make, facilitating concentration of spares, skills and equipment.

The branches are:

Sofia Goroublyane	- Mercedes Benz
Sofia Hadji Dimitar	- Mercedes Benz
Pazardjik (Plovdiv)	- Mercedes Benz
Bourgas	- Volvo
Russe	- Fiat/Iveco Ford
Vidin	- Renault

Each branch depot has responsibilities to provide trucks suitable for transport, and to undertake cleaning, maintenance and minor repair. The six depots are located close to the major regions of export generation:

Bourgas	-	is the major Bulgarian port
Vidin	-	is the major Danube port
Russe	-	is a major industrial area and en route to Eastern Europe
Pazerdjik	-	is a major industrial area and on the main West Europe - Near Middle East route
Sofia	-	is the capital city, on the main crosstrade route, and a major industrial area.

Truck composition consists of about 1200 reefers used mainly for agricultural and food products; 2600 normal tilt trucks for various uses; and about 150 specials including tankers, container chassis and heavy lift vehicles.

In terms of markets, So-mat have a far larger fleet of vehicles than Bulgarian bilateral trade alone merits, and the company has developed its fleet based on its activities in the cross-trades. The rules of agreements on cross-trading in Europe almost universally require the cross-trader to pass through the home territory 'en-route' to its destination. Bulgaria's geographical location is particularly beneficial in this respect as it is located midway between the main markets of West Europe and the Near and Middle East - both hard currency generators.

As a result, from 1970 in particular, there has been a deliberate state policy to concentrate upon this market. In 1975, the number of So-mat trucks was more than doubled by purchasing some 2,500 vehicles in one order, with the aim of developing the cross-trade market.

Second to this cross-trading activity is that of serving the Bulgarian import and export trade which is and always has been relatively limited in size and in its demands for road transport.

However, cross-trading presents a number of problems - in particular relating to the volatile politics of the Near and Middle East. The two main markets by far in this region are, and always have been Iran and Iraq, which together account for 80-90% of the traffic - split approximately 50% each. The remaining 10-20% originates from, or is destined for Kuwait, Jordan, Lebanon, Syria, Afghanistan or Pakistan. In recent years political problems have disturbed the main markets of Iran and Iraq - not least the Gulf war and recently the Gulf crisis. The latter was predicted by the end of 1990, to have cost So-mat $18m in lost traffic, and directly $4m in loss of vehicles and an account held in a Kuwaiti bank.

Road transport, however, is a very important mode to the Near and Middle East from Europe. The infrastructure is adequate, if not good; the Near and Middle East market is poorly organised and insecure and road transport offers continuous protection and assured delivery, whilst ports are poorly located and far less orientated West than East.

Saudi Arabia is not a market destination, as the Saudis have consistently refused to allow East European trucks into their territory as part of an anti-Socialist policy. Diplomatic changes currently taking place may alter this. An indirect result is that the UAE is also absent from So-mat's market, as road links are available only through Saudi Arabia.

In Western Europe, 50% of all traffic originates from, or is destined for West Germany. Quotas are easy to acquire for cross-trading from West Germany - unlike France and the Benelux countries in particular, which are very protective of their trucking industries. However, bilateral agreements do exist with all West and East European countries, although some are much more flexible in applying them than others - for example, the UK applies no quota restrictions at all. So-mat operates services to all European countries, in varying frequently and regularity. After West Germany, the markets of Austria and France (despite quota restrictions) are the biggest.

Unaccompanied loads are not frequently undertaken as one of the major benefits of trucking is driver accompaniment to a load. Unaccompanied loads are used only in two circumstances:

- when quotas are restricted
- when contracts specify otherwise, and So-mat shipping is used.

So-mat owns two sea-going ro-ro vessels which trade between Bourgas on the Black Sea coast, and the western coastline of Europe - for example, Cork (Eire), Barcelona (Spain), Porto (Portugal) Marseille (France), Morocco and Bristol (UK). Typical coastal trade is deep-frozen meat from Eire to Iran, loaded on trailers and accompanied by road from Bulgaria to Tehran. The main problem is backloads. Bristol was once included in the schedule because of a contract to carry potatoes from Cyprus to the UK. Now that this has ceased, fruit between Morocco and France is carried.

Two Danube ro-ro vessels are also owned carrying forty nine trucks each. The main trade route is from Vidin in North-West Bulgaria to Linz (Austria) and Passau (West Germany). This helps to overcome Austrian controls on quotas and environmental constraints and hence is both practically and politically a very important service.

So-mat is the only international haulier in East Europe to own ships, partly at least because a very large haulier is required to fill such vessels and provide adequate capital for their purchase and replacement.

The East European market is not important to So-mat who deliberately aim to avoid East European transit whenever possible. Most East European journeys are left to other competing truck companies based in Bulgaria, or the bilateral partner companies (eg Pekaes; Romtrans etc). The main reason for this is that up to now, payment has been largely in barter, or in 'transferable roubles' - both of which are almost useless to So-mat. Costs remain largely West European (including truck maintenance and depreciation), but the revenue cannot offset this.

In total, East European traffic amounts to about 10-15% of the total, of which USSR traffic dominates, followed far behind by that to and from Poland, Czechoslovakia, Hungary and lastly Romania. However, from 1 January 1991, all intra-CMEA trade will have to be paid for in hard currency and consequently the attitude of hauliers such as So-mat, to East European traffic, may change.

So-mat also owns a number of other companies both in Bulgaria and abroad. In Sofia and Dragoman (close to the Yugoslav border and on the main trade route) there are companies totally owned by So-mat that specialise in the heavy repair and maintenance of trucks. The services at these two companies are available to any trucking company, although the majority of their work is carried out for So-mat trucks. Other users must pay a commercial rate in hard currency, including these established in Bulgaria.

In Sofia there is another company producing parts for trucks, especially springs and bolts, contracted from West European suppliers. These parts are mainly destined for So-mat trucks, but are available to others for hard currency.

In Dragoman a joint venture has been set up with Schmidt Trailers of West Germany to assemble semi-trailers. Production is sold to So-mat and occasionally to other East and West European trucking companies, once again for hard currency. Eventually the plant will not just assemble but will produce fully, trailers to a Schmidt design.

At present each of these companies are operated as a part of So-mat, and there is no organisational or financial independence. In time it is planned to introduce an element of independence with each company having to operate separately and survive within a competitive, commercial market. Abroad So-mat have a number of company interests. There are three trucking companies - Vienna Transport (Austria) which has been operating since 1980 between West Europe and the Middle and Near East; Libutco (Libya) which concentrates on the transport of grain from agricultural centres to the ports of Libya for 90% of its traffic and the remainder is general trucking work to and from Tunisia; and the Kuwaiti-Baghdad Trucking Company which began operations in the late 1970's working between Kuwait and Iraq. This latter company has ceased operation since the Gulf crisis.

A number of other companies are either part or fully owned. 'Demand' of Austria is 96% owned by Somat with the remainder held by the original Austrian owner. It is a freight-forwarding company providing services both for So-mat and others. 'Demand' also looks after So-mat vehicles in Western Europe monitoring their progress, co-ordinating trucks and loads, and finding backhauls. It also clears in advance So-mat loads at customs check-points, thus facilitating transit across Europe.

DLN of Regensburg (West Germany) is a forwarding company with a joint shareholder in West Germany. It also provides local management of ro-ro vessels owned by So-mat and used on the Danube.

IBTC of Tehran (Iran) is a forwarding company used to acquire backhauls to Western and Eastern Europe in the cross-trade market.

Meanwhile, a number of other West German joint ventures are to be established by the end of 1990, but actual details were not available at the time of writing.

Overall, the overseas network is aimed at directly supporting the cross-trading activities of So-mat, and a network of representatives and agents are located at the major ports and export/import generating centres of Western Europe, and through the Middle and Near East. The progress in developing this network in recent years is nothing short of phenomenal. It is worth remembering that it was not until 1989 that Bulgarian companies had easy access to the international telephone network - and yet just over one year later So-mat has a dedicated company in Austria looking after its vehicles throughout Western Europe. It is also worth noting that the representatives of So-mat in Europe and the Near-Middle East, are not used as 'salesmen' but merely represent the company locally. All traffic is acquired through freight forwarders - albeit some of them largely So-mat owned.

Hard currency remains the driving force behind the So-mat industry. The vast majority of So-mat income is in a convertible form and hence there are few problems, compared with many other Bulgarian industries, of acquiring resources. The only local leva income is obtained from domestic services and even this is useful in purchasing local materials and facilities and for paying local salaries. In fact, even some services provided to Bulgarians in Bulgaria are done so on hard currency terms.

The state still controls almost all banks in Bulgaria, although attempts are currently underway to create a private banking sector. All so-mat hard currency earnings have to pass through the Bulgarian Foreign Trade Bank where the state retains a part as taxation. Of the remainder, part of the hard currency has to be converted to Bulgarian leva at the official rate. The remaining hard currency is retained by the state for So-mat to re-use as it wishes - within Bulgarian law. The unit of currency is chosen by So-mat and financiers within the company swap currencies to maximise profitability.

This process is a considerable improvement upon that which existed prior to 1 January 1990 when all hard currency was converted to 'transferable leva' and then reconverted to hard currency when So-mat gained permission for the expenditure they wished to make. At that time, no profits could be made by So-mat from the currency markets and the State had a very strong say in every investment decision.

Privatisation is currently part of a popular debate in Bulgaria with the state, local population and within So-mat itself. Some moves have been made in a number of industries (for example, banking and the development of independent hauliers) but none as yet by the state to privatise So-mat itself. This may reflect the general policies of the Socialist government at present. So-mat does have a number of clear ideas about privatisation and intends to go ahead when possible, to create an umbrella company with the operating companies reconstituted independently beneath it. However, the timescale remains uncertain and is likely to be relatively long-term.

Competition in the haulage market of Bulgaria remains very limited. What there is consists of:

(i)   National hauliers, Autotransport, who have almost without exception, extended their activities into the international field. However, they are involved solely in the bilateral trades as they lack the necessary infrastructure and modern technology to enter the cross-trade market to any extent. Quality of service is restricted, in that very few West European trucks are owned and those that are, are restricted to So-mat used vehicles. Both East and West Europe is covered with a dominance of the former. West European destinations tend to be restricted to West Germany, Yugoslavia, Greece, Italy and Austria.

(ii)   There are also a small but growing number of independent hauliers, most commonly one truck, one man, commonly operating East or West trucks of considerable age. No co-operatives exist in the haulage sector of Bulgaria. The independents face an unsure future as they rely on loads rejected by others, and hence ultimately on the buoyancy of the Bulgarian economy.

The minimum legal wage in Bulgaria is two hundred leva a month. International So-mat drivers receive a standard 395 leva a month. On top of this they also receive a hard currency daily allowance whilst travelling abroad in the West or Near/Middle East which includes a hotel allowance commonly retained by the drivers whilst they sleep in the cab! The hard currency allowance is a standard 50DM a day, regardless of destination, to cover food, accommodation and other expenses (not fuel), which is a maximum allowable under Bulgarian law. In addition, drivers receive a bonus in hard currency if they return earlier than the standard trip home, or if they carry a backhaul.

On average a driver works twenty days a month but those who are particularly keen and efficient may work twenty five days and can receive maximum bonuses. In this case the maximum payment to a driver might be $700-800 a month on top of his leva payment. Most, of course, receive less.

So-mat has a responsibility under the CMR convention, to be insured. The state does not subsidise insurance, directly at least, and So-mat must pay all premiums. Insurance of both truck and load is exercised through the Bulgarian National Insurance Company (state owned) which re-insures through the West. Recently, to reduce premium payments, So-mat have insured only half their trucks and have used their own resources to cover the rest, through a specific fund. The cargoes will remain covered by CMR. One proud boast of So-mat is that in thirty years they have never lost a cargo.

The only taxation paid by So-mat is taken as part of hard currency profits, and consequently income determines the absolute level of taxation paid, and not vehicle usage. There is no vehicle, fuel or purchase tax paid, resulting in considerably lower tax burdens than in the West.

Current diesel prices (September 1990) are 1.60 leva/litre (about twenty pence). So-mat have their own guaranteed supplies - vital at this time of fuel shortages - but at the same price as everyone else. Fuel for vehicles from abroad is available only with hard currency coupons and queuing is a necessity. Clearly fuel is cheaper than in the West, but this advantage is restricted as the majority of kilometres are covered in other countries.

As So-mat is mainly involved in the cross-trade market, few competitions from abroad are of concern to them. The main external competition is the Turks who operate effectively and extensively on the Western Europe-Near/ Middle East cross-trades. They possess a number of advantages in competing with So-mat:

- Turkey is located on the main West Europe-Near/Middle East trade route;
- they are able to transit Turkey for a longer distance than So-mat can transit Bulgaria;
- they have a greater export market to West Europe.

Despite these advantages they remain in second place to So-mat. In 1989, Turkish trucks made 10,000 trips to the Middle and Near East; So-mat made 16,000.

Pekaes of Poland were important on the cross-trading routes until the recent growth of bilateral trade which has forced them to concentrate elsewhere due to constraints in capacity. Meanwhile, the Soviet Union remains a significant competitor, particularly in the Iranian market, travelling from the Soviet Union for a large distance 'en route' - where fuel is available to them at only six kopecs to the litre. Other East Europeans are not major competitors - for example, Romtrans provide no real competition despite a similar geographical location to Bulgaria, largely because of poor organisation and quality of service. So-mat even undertake journeys for Romtrans on occasions.

In discussion with So-mat's senior managers, they were at particular pains to emphasise that under the 1975 state decree, So-mat has to be a profitable hard currency earner. If unprofitable, the law allows for its reconstitution - but not bankruptcy, yet. There are no state controls on the services it provides and hence it can and must price commercially. However, we should note that there are price constraints on the services it consumes - fuel, telephones, energy, land, buildings and so on. Wages paid to drivers are not so different from Western Europe as is commonly claimed; the highest paid drivers receive, in total, the equivalent of about $1,000 a month.

So-mat emphasised that Bulgarian international haulage was continuously criticised for being state owned and therefore, subsidised. In practice, So-mat is not directly. Meanwhile, the French government refuse extra quotas to So-mat, despite the latter's ability to carry three times the traffic they do at present. This, claim So-mat, can only harm French interests as French haulage prices are higher. French hauliers are also unwilling to travel to the Near and Middle East as there are few rewards for them. Quota increases would be a quick and easy way to encourage both the French and Bulgarian economies, and harm no-one.

Some Conclusions

(i)   So-mat is the largest road haulier in the world and also in the East-West trade of Europe. They are a relatively well organised company, struggling to develop and expand in an international market, constrained by the internal limitations of Bulgaria, and the absence of a sound economy.

(ii)   So-mat is the archetypal cross-trader, which accounts for the large majority of its activities and for its size as a company. Consequently, despite its size, its concentration on the cross-trades means that it has posed less of a threat to West European hauliers, who are more commonly involved in the bilateral trades. However, in partially monopolising the cross-trades between West Germany and the Near-Middle East in particular, it does present fierce competition in that market to Western hauliers.

(iii)   So-mat remains heavily involved with the state. It is 100% state controlled, with few prospects of privatisation in the near or even medium term future. The Bulgarian state remains socialist (communist) controlled, with a strong commitment to the old policies of state interference and ownership. Despite these constraints, So-mat has attempted to become as commercial and competitive as it can, and consequently has invested exclusively in Western trucks.

(iv)   Hard currency remains the driving force behind So-mat's activities, remaining under an obligation to produce hard currency profits. Consequently, markets where hard currency is not generated are avoided whenever possible. Thus East Europe and the domestic market are only covered when either unavoidable, as part of a bigger contract, or trucks would otherwise remain idle, and marginal costs are covered. Both the East European and domestic markets are left to the limited competition from national and independent hauliers.

(v)   There is no evidence of direct subsidy to So-mat in the form of cash payments. However, there is perhaps the strongest evidence in East Europe of indirect subsidy either through the provision of state services to the company at lower than hire cost (for example, tele- phones, electricity, fuel etc), or through the vague movements of finance between arms of the So-mat organisation. No proper accounts are published.

(vi)   So-mat possesses a very advanced network of representatives in Western Europe, the Near and Middle East, unrivalled by other East European trucking companies, and superior to most West European operators. Undoubtedly this network forms the basis of the So-mat growth in cross-trading, forming strong links with potential importers and exporters and acquiring extensive backhauls. In this area, So-mat is very well organised and advanced in its attitudes and approach.

(vii)   So-mat have not been slow in extending their Western interests by the acquisition and development of affiliate and joint ventures, giving them a foothold in the European Community prior to 1992, and enabling them to monitor their trucks whilst in the West of Europe and the Near and Middle East. Further acquisitions in Germany in late 1990 will extend their presence in the Europe of post 1992.

(viii)   So-mat are likely to retain their stronghold in the cross-trade markets despite the growth in Turkish involvement - simply because of their network of representatives, their relatively high level of quality of service, the size of their operation, their ability to undercut others due to a combination of cheap wages, insurance and tax, and a relatively high level of state involvement and indirect subsidy. The need to earn hard currency for the foreseeable future remains a great stimulus to their continued presence in this market.

(ix)   In the immediate future, So-mat represents a large, relatively well-organised haulage company, struggling to shed its old shackles of Communist state involvement. Despite these sizeable constraints it has developed a specific market and provides a relatively high level of quality of service within it. However, the company is in need of Western training and advice to improve its financial accounting procedures, its level of technology and its ability to manage and organise. Without such developments it cannot hope to compete with the improvements occurring in Western hauliers, or with the developments at Hungarocamion in Eastern Europe.

6 Czechoslovakia

Introduction and Background

Czechoslovakia had been a Communist controlled State until the changes of 1989 and 1990, since 1948, and a member of the CMEA from that year, to this day. Since 1 January 1969, it has been governed under a federal constitution under which Slovakia enjoys equal status to the Czech speaking regions of Bohemia and Moravia. Where there was formerly one government, there are now three, although the federal government makes all important economic decisions and, by means of Federal Ministries, retains direct control over large sections of the economy. The Federal government has its seat in Prague as does the Czech State government; the Slovak State government has its seat in Bratislava.

The total area of Czechoslovakia is about 127,900 sq km. The country is bounded by the Soviet Union, Poland, the DDR, West Germany, Austria and Hungary, and is divided into three main regions - the Czech speaking Bohemia and Moravia in the west and centre; and the Slovak speaking Slovakia in the east.

Although Czechoslovakia is a land locked country it has access to the sea through its two main rivers; the Elbe, which flows north through the

DDR to the North sea, and the Danube which flows through Hungary, Yugoslavia and Romania to the Black Sea. Both carry considerable import and export traffic, offering an alternative mode to road, rail or air, and include a number of roll on/roll off vessels carrying trucks, trailers and containers in limited numbers.

Population at 1 January, 1988 was estimated at about 15.5m, of whom 10.3m were in Bohemia and Moravia, and 5.2m in Slovakia. The main centres of population are Prague (Bohemia) (1.2m), the capital and major industrial and commercial centre; Brno (Moravia), (390000); Brakslava (Slovakia) (430000); Ostrava (Moravia) (330000); Plsen (Bohemia) (175000) and Kosice (Slovakia) (230000).

A large proportion of Czech trade is conducted with the East European countries of the CMEA, particularly the USSR with whom Czechoslovakia have the strongest economic ties of Eastern European countries. Recent polical and economic changes have done little to alter this as yet, partly at least because of currency convertability problems. However, apart from trade with other CMEA members, there is also notable trade with West Germany, Austria, Switzerland, Italy, France and the UK.

Until the changes of 1989 and 1990, economic development has always been implemented through a continuous series of five year plans, the last of which had emphasised specialisation in certain products to meet CMEA overall plans for the Eastern Bloc. Much of these plans has now been abandoned in the moves away from central planning and towards a free market economy. In 1988 and 1989, Czechoslovakia had a very small balance of payments deficit with the West, whilst the international debts were amongst the smallest of the Eastern Bloc.

Prior to the market changes now taking place, the Czechoslovakian government had introduced its own restructuring of traditional economic mechanisms which had been followed during the 1950's, 1960's, 1970's and into the 1980's. Foreign Trade Organisations (State owned monopolies controlling import and export of all items), were allowed to expand activities, many State enterprises were acquiring the rights to conduct their own foreign trade, and a whole middle tier of managerial beaurocracy was being phased out. These reforms were only partially completed when the changes of 1989 began to occur. Consequently, there is currently a mix of unreformed, partially reformed and wholly reformed industry and agriculture, some of which was reformed prior to the developments of 1989/90, some since. Much confusion and uncertainty remains affecting all industrial sectors, including trucking.

All Czechoslovakian industry and agriculture, barring very few exceptions, is nationalised including the trucking sector, although plans are now advanced to begin mass privatisation in the coming years. Consequently, the international trucking industry has had to develop in the framework of State ownership, and all the familiar East European constraints on prices, investments, employment, wages, management and so on. It has also benefitted from both direct and indirect subsidy to a level that remains largely unknown, even by those directly involved in the management of the business.

Like all East European International trucking, Czechoslovakian State involvement has been largely aimed at earning hard currency and indirectly to provide transport for Czechoslovakian exports and imports. All this is about to change, although the earning of hard currency remains an important issue as the Czechoslovakian crown remains unconvertible for the next few years at least. State policy is now to remove their involvement (and subsidy) from industry, to encourage market forces to predominate, and thus to expose international trucking (amongst other industries) to true competition. As we shall see, this is a formidable ambition as little progress has yet been made in this direction. Until 1989, Czechoslovakia was one of the hard line socialist states and few economic reforms had been carried out - certainly very few in comparison with its neighbours, Hungary and Poland.

CESMAD International Trucking

We can now go on to examine the role of Czechoslovakian international trucking in the East-West European road haulage market. Much of what is outlined and analysed below was derived from discussions with the Director of CESMAD, the Czechoslovakian International Trucking Company, Jiri Kladiva, in Prague in July, 1990.

CESMAD is the Czechoslovakian road haulage group, which remains a hundred percent State owned, and until the 1970s held a monopoly in operation of road freight services to, from and within the State. It was set up in 1966 to operate all international road freight journeys whenever possible, into and out of Czechoslovakia, in a form and for reasons, that were the same throughout Eastern Europe.

Meanwhile, the CSAD, national only road freight operating companies, had been establised in 1948 after the advent of the socialist regime - and have been used since 1966 to provide the international truck fleet for CESMAD when necessary.

CESMAD is actually an umbrella holding company under which there are eleven truck operating companies (CSAD's) that represent each of the states' eleven regions (counties). Each operating company covers its own geographical area for both national and international traffic, and tends to restrict itself to that area, although legally it can attract traffic and market itself elsewhere throughout the country.

In the past, and until very recently, the operating companies cross subsidised one another, the efficient helping to support the inefficient. But from 1 November 1990, each operating company will be run as a totally separate concern and will be transferred into one of eleven limited companies, with shareholders which may include organisations and industries other than the State. This privatisation process will end any possibility of cross-subsidisation, and will force each operating company more into the commercial world for both national and international operations. The eleven companies at July 1990 are listed in Table 10, each working under the name CSAD (Czechoslovakia Stratria Automobilova Doprava) - the same organisations that operatre regional public transport in Czechoslovakia, with the same structure as found in much of Eastern Europe.

No-one has yet announced how shareholders will be found, and the sale of the CSAD companies could be to industry, organiations, employees or even to the State itself - or a mix.

Privatisation is a result of new legislation introduced from 1 June 1990, that requires all State owned industries (except for a few very strategic ones) to be sold and set up as limited companies. After privat- isation, CESMAD will be retained as an umbrella group, financed by each of the CSAD companies, to provide policy and direction, overseas representation, co-ordination and more. Both CESMAD and CSAD road freight operators receive no direct subsidy - it is claimed. The public transport operations of CSAD are heavily subsidised by the State, begging the question, whether these subsidies 'drift' into the road freight sector through joint staffing, technical facilities and so on?

Overall CESMAD has responsibility for over 3000 trucks through its

CSAD subsidiares used for both national and international work. The majority are employed in the former sector, of course, but vehicles are largely interchangeable and, therefore, it is impossible to be exact about the international fleet size. However, it is widely recognised that it is notably smaller than that of Hungary, Bulgaria and Poland.

In the future, the eleven companies will co-operate but at a cost - and all services provided will be charged for accordingly (maintenance, servicing, lease and hiring, cleaning and so on).

Each CSAD company has a number of operating depots to serve both the national and international markets - commonly between nine and fourteen for each company. At present, trucks are rarely transferred between depots, but this may become increasingly common as privitasation bites.

CESMAD provides much more than just international haulage services through its contacts with the CSAD companies, and as a seperate organisation in its own right. Eight spheres of activity other than international road freighting, but related to it, can be identified:

(i)   Forwarding and organising international haulage. Close relations in freight markets are maintained with twenty three other foreign countries, producing data on future freight contracts and truck movements. CESMAD thus provides a road freight broker service for all companies, including CSADs.

(ii)   General services for international haulage including permit provision, passport and visa services, customs documentation (including TIR carnets, AGT manifests, CMR consignment notes etc.,) fuel credit services through Shell, DKV' and UTA, and VIA card credit services for road tolls.

(iii)   Legal and insurance assistance. Monitoring and application of CMR, TIR, AETR, ADR and ATP conventions; legal services such as representation, police communication, assistance at times of traffic accident etc; assistance over damages and for claims; co-operation with unions; and advisory services.

(iv)   Financial and convertible currency services. This includes - financial settlements abroad; VAT reimbursement;

guarantees; invoicing services; loan and advance payments; currency transactions for the import of trucks and other equipment and spare parts; exchange of currency; financial advice; provision of convertible currency for other Czechoslovakian hauliers abroad.

(v)   Customs assistance. Co-operation and liasion with customs officers at home and abroad; and customs guarantees for foreign trucks in Czechoslovakia.

(vi)   Import and technical aid. A whole range of services related to truck and spare parts imports, including negotiations with foreign suppliers over prices, technical specifications etc; technical help over truck repairs, and servicing etc.

(vii)   Professional education. Professional training of haulage managers, customs officers and drivers in financial services, inter- national regulations, dangerous goods movements, social rules of driving and so on.

These CESMAD services are likely to be developed and marketed as part of the privatisation, market orientation process in Czechoslovakia, in the coming years.

Each operating company is between 200-400 vehicles in size and thus comparable in operation and market share. In international terms, twenty three countries are served (1990) including almost all of Europe, and limited parts of the Near and Middle East, particularly Iraq and Syria.

However, the largest part of the market now lies in Western Europe, estimated to be the origin and destination of 70% of all loads. The major destinations are the ports of Eastern Europe - particularly Hamburg, Bremen, Antwerp, Rotterdam and Trieste, but many others as well. In East Europe the main destinations (clearly for onward travel by sea) are Gdansk and Szczecin in Poland.

In terms of countries served, undoubtedly the main market for both final destinations and port related shipments, is West Germany followed well behind by Belgium and the Netherlands - including their port traffic which moves on to the USA, UK, Eire, Japan and beyond. Well below these three destinations are Italy, Austria, France and Scandinavia, whilst

TABLE 10 : CSAD OPERATING COMPANIES, JULY 1990

CSAD	KNV	Pratia
CSAD	np	Ceske Budejovice
CSAD	np	Plzen
CSAD	np	Usti nad Labern
CSAD	np	Hradec kralove
CSAD	np	Brno
CSAD	np	Ostrava
CSAD	np	Bratislava
CSAD	np	Banska Bystrica
CSAD	np	Kosice
CSAD	np	hl m. Prahy

Source : CESMAD

Spain, Portugal and the UK are served only infrequently, albeit with regular shipments.

Eastern Bloc traffic is much smaller in quantity and frequency than that to Western Europe. The main trading partner by road is claimed to be the Soviet Union, contrasting with the position in Hungary and Poland, where road transit is dominated by Soviet hauliers. Polish port traffic is also very important, whilst there are notable, if not large, quantities of traffic to and from Hungary and the DDR. Both Romania and Bulgaria are noted for backhauls only on trips returning from Turkey, the Near and Middle East and elsewhere.

The Near and Middle East market is now really only a 'symbolic' one. The Iran/Iraq war destroyed the international road freight sector and it has never recovered. In 1975, CESMAD was sending 300 trucks a month to various destinations in Iran, Iraq, Syria, Jordan, the Lebanon and Kuwait - now it is more normal to send five or six.

Sources of traffic are varied within Czechoslovakia with the majority of traffic emanating through contacts between CESMAD and the State run FTO's, of which some forty exist. These FTO's no longer have a monopoly on foreign trade as under reforms initiated in 1988, many State enterprises now have the right to conduct foreign trade with companies abroad, directly, and thus organise their own road freight transport. However, despite these changes, FTO's remain dominent, independent parties within the international trading structure, albeit still State owned, and remain the main source of CESMAD export and import traffic. Since both the FTO's and CESMAD are State controlled (until November 1990) the independence of transport contracts between the two must be doubted. Some form of hidden subsidy is almost inevitable, if only in the form of traffic direction.

Other sources of traffic are the productive State industries themselves, and a variety of independent and co-operative ventures. Neither of these sectors produces a great proportion of CESMAD traffic as yet, although it is growing rapidly from a small base.

In Western Europe, backhauls are obtained largely through the network of representatives and agents, and the nine offices maintained in West Germany, Austria, Sweden, the Netherlands and Yugoslavia.

However, many loads are attracted through the policy of industries and FTO's selling CIF and importing FOB - thus controlling transport and being able to dictate the haulier and its nationality (in this case CESMAD whenever possible). This CIF/FOB practice is a common one in Eastern Europe and effectively helps to control a large proportion of road haulage between East and West and vice versa.

Somewhere between 65 and 70% of all CSAD trucks are manufactured by Liaz (Skoda) in Czechoslovakia, and are used on both national and international work. The remaining 30-35% are entirely of western manufacture, chosen because of their technical superiority; the fact that many journeys take place almost entirely in Western Europe; there are few if any repair, service or maintenance facilities specifically for Liaz trucks in the west; and costs of operating Liaz trucks are higher in the long term. Western trucks also present a strong marketing advantage.

Western manufactured vehicles are used as exclusively as possible on Western European routes. In fact, CESMAD would like to purchase a larger number of their trucks, but recent economic changes, including the 15% devaluation of the Crown in 1990, has meant that the cost of western products has risen even faster than usual, thus making acquisition that much more difficult.

Western vehicles operated include Renault, Iveco/Ford and Volvo. No Mercedes are used as they are felt to be too expensive compared with the benefits they bring additional to competitive makes. One problem soon to confront CESMAD is that a very large contract for Volvos was entered into in 1983, and all the new trucks then purchased are now up for renewal. The cost involved in the current economic conditions is large and unaffordable - yet no other solution seems possible.

Liaz trucks are rarely used for more than four years in international work, whilst Western made trucks are still frequently operating after seven or eight years. When trucks are too old for international work they tend to be cascaded down through national duties until they are completely exhausted, or are sold to private industries and co-operatives, a little earlier than this.

Traditionally, the exports of Czechoslovakia have always covered a very broad spectrum of industrial and agricultural output as the county has long been very diversified in its economic structure. Geographically, the goods emerge from many areas as there is a notable scatter of industry and agriculture from East to West. This compares favourably with the distribution of economic activity in (for example) Poland and Hungary, where concentrations of industry are far more pronounced.

Generally speaking, manufacturing industry has been the greater strength in the Czechoslovakian economy, but agriculture is relatively highly mechanised for the Eastern Bloc. The main crops are cereals, sugar beet, potatoes, fruit and vegetables, wildstock and dairy produce. Much of this is exported.

Czechoslovakia, meanwhile, is poorly endowed with natural resources and depends on the USSR for many raw materials. This may, of course, change in time but remains the case in 1990. Nevertheless, Czechoslovakia is highly industrialised with, until late 1990, all investment and development controlled by the State. This has been particularly chanelled into heavy industry (especially vehicles, iron and steel, electronics and various by products), although traditional industries of textiles, clothing, leather and footwear, glass and ceramics, and timber and wood products have continued to expand. Much of the output is exported once again.

In terms of Czechoslovakian international trucking, commodities carried tend to reflect the pattern of imports and exports generally. Exports carried by CESMAD include glass, textiles, clothes, metal industrial products, wood industrial products, food and malt. Commodities imported and carried by CESMAD, are also broad in character and include in particular, high-tech goods, food, chemicals, raw materials and consumer products.

Backhauls are kept as high as possible deliberately as with all haulage companies, or else, quite simply, no profit would be made. This is particularly true on the longer routes - for example to Spain, Portugal and the Near/Middle East.

The level of attraction of backhaul, varies with the route chosen - for West Germany, it is on average about 60%, whilst for CESMAD as a whole something between 50 and 60% is a more normal level. UK backhaul averages are higher although total journey numbers are considerably lower than West Germany. The UK represents a fairly long trip for CESMAD and thus a high backhaul rate is needed. As noted earlier, most backhauls in Western Europe are obtained through agents and representatives to whom CESMAD drivers must report to ascertain backhaul availability whilst abroad.

International drivers with CESMAD, receive as part of their incomes, a proportion in hard currency used both as a 'perk', and as a necessity for them to survive on the road in the West. The result is that the job of international drivers is viewed with some envy, particularly whilst the Czechoslovakian Crown remains unconvertible. Even if paid all in Crowns, it would still be a well paid occupation, adding to its status and popularity.

Consequently, CESMAD and the State can afford to impose quite severe restrictions on those who are permitted to enter the international driving sector. Each potential driver:

- must have driven trucks of 32,000kg or more, laden weight, for at least five years;
- must be mature, ie at least twenty one. CESMAD average age for drivers at the start of their international careers is twenty seven;
- must be healthy;
- must have trained especially for the job including passing a series of psychological tests.

Retirement age in Czechoslovakia is normally sixty. After fifty, truck drivers are subject to an annual health test. Actual retirement age depends on the local depot manager who can decide when to move a driver from international work before he reaches sixty. In many cases, drivers are rotated between international and national driving to give more employees the benefits of overseas travel and work. CESMAD's own internal official retirement age is now fifty five, but due to employee resistance this is flexibily applied.

Incentive schemes relating to wages do exist, but for safety reasons are restricted. Standard trip times are calculated in days and hard currency is paid accordingly. Driver records are monitored constantly to ensure that drivers do not abuse the system by either travelling too slowly or too quickly.

All vehicles, drivers and loads must be insured under Czechoslovakian laws, but CESMAD only insure up the the minumum required through the CMR convention and third party agreements. Theft problems in Italy and France require additional insurance, and extra premuiums are payable in the Near and Middle East. Generally speaking, premiums are considerably lower than in the West at the moment but may increase dramatically, to rather more commercial rates, as the Czechoslovakian economy becomes more market orientated.

Road vehicle taxation does not exist in Czechoslovakia, but all vehicle operating companies, including the CSAD's are taxed according to the kilometrage their vehicles cover each year. Plans are being prepared by the State for some form of road vehicle tax in the near future.

Fuel prices are low by West European standards at 7.5 Crowns a litre (1990) (about 60-70p). This price is about double that of 1989, but looks to remain stable for some time. Clearly, this fuel price advantage is only of limited value to the Czechoslovakian international hauliers who are restricted as all foreign companies are, by various fuel import laws in West Europe - particularly West Germany. However, within Czechoslovakia, western hauliers cannot benefit from lower fuel prices, as fuel is available only for hard currency or credit (payable in hard currency), at prohibitively expensive exchange rates.

EAST-WEST ROAD TRANSPORT, EASTBOUND AND WESTBOUND, BY NATIONALITY OF THE HAULIER

Road transport (Westbound), by nationality of the haulier, between the state trading countries of Eastern Europe and the EC, 1985, in tonnes

State Trading Countries of Eastern Europe	EC Hauliers from country of origin %		EC Hauliers from country of destination %		Cross-trading Hauliers %		Total Road Transport in tonnes
USSR	457944	64	248054	35	10416	1	716414
Poland	277381	23	807545	67	112684	9	1197610
GDR	2043694	50	1905968	47	91929	2	4041591
Czechoslovakia	1116348	54	861891	42	72194	3	2050433
Hungary	534551	51	307730	29	192761	18	1035042
Bulgaria	120343	62	55687	28	16611	9	192641
Rumania	369354	56	270704	41	19274	2	659332
TOTAL	4919615	49	4457579	45	515869	5	9893063

Unlike both Poland and Hungary, there is very little competition in international road haulage from and to Czechoslovakia. Until the mid-1970's there was none at all, with CESMAD operating through CSAD, a total state monopoly.

Competition since then has been allowed and it has grown from nothing but only to a very small level. One reason for this is that unlike Hungary, the national and international trucking company has always been one and the same - and hence there has been no apportunity for the national trucking company to diversify into international trucking in competition with other State companies.

The main sectors providing competition are:

- independents   (1-5 trucks generally)
- co-operatives   (of all sizes)
- own account trucks from industry and agriculture.

There is no direct State competition, although of course, at the moment, own account transport is effectively State owned.

The future of the small company competitors does not look too promising. In the 1970's and 1980's, international trucking looked a very interesting and exciting way of earning a living, enabling the driver to obtain a scarce visa and passport and access to hard currency. These problems are now declining and so, therefore, are the attractions. The Czechoslovakian economy is undoubtedly heading for difficult times as the Crown is devalued and market forces have their way.

Overall it was estimated that CESMAD's share of trucking based in Czechoslovakia was about 75%. Although initially, this does not sound all that high, the remaining 25% was mainly own account agricultural traffic with other forms of competition making up a very small proportion. The agricultural sector is not a true competitor as it has its own monopolies in certain areas and specialisations - but it is a major source of international transport for commodities which might otherwise travel by CESMAD, independents or co-operatives.

Czechoslovakia suffers from complex hard currency rules as does most of East Europe. Meanwhile, one of the main reasons for the introduction and development of CESMAD was supply to attract hard currency to Czechoslovakia, and to reduce hard currency expenditure on transport provided by West Europeans. It is for this reason that the CIF/FOB. sale/purchase, export/import pattern of trade exists.

With an unconvertible Crown, hard currency remains a vital commodity which the State uses to purchase Western goods and services and individuals use to purchase the luxuries of life, and to travel. To control hard currency and to obtain as much as possible for its own purposes, the State has a multitude of regulations relating to convertible currency. In terms of CESMAD they work in the following way:

(i)   CESMAD acts as an accountant in calculating the total hard currency needs of the CSAD's operations for the forthcoming financial year - this has to include such purchases in the West, new western vehicles, subsistence for drivers, etc.

(ii)   CESMAD estimates the hard currency revenues for the same year.

(iii)   These two figures are compared to give a ratio of hard currency revenue to expenditure.

(iv)   This financial information is presented to the Czechoslovakian State Bank who check its accuracy and evaluate the estimates made.

(v)   The State Bank provides the hard currency needed to cover the total costs of the CSAD operating companies - assuming it approves the package as a whole.

(vi)   If CESMAD, in the form of the CSAD operating companies, do better than their approved estimates, then they can keep any residue to invest largely as they wish, within general State rules. They also keep any surplus of hard currency revenue over costs. If they do not achieve their estimates then they must make up the loss somehow - normally by investing less in new western vehicles. Consequently, there is a fairly strong incentive to meet hard currency estimates and to increase hard currency earnings where possible.

This procedure is basically the same for all potential hard currency earning industries currently under State ownership. As privatisation looms, it is presumed that the regulations will become less onerous and the opportunities to earn and invest hard currency, that much greater. It remains at present, beaurocratic, slow and open to a number of questionable and dubious practices, including that of over-estimating hard currency needs by CESMAD, and others relating to target assessment and calculation of profits. One partial solution to these malpractices, would be to allow industries (including international trucking) to retain more of the hard currency earned - if not all - so that they could decide themselves how much hard currency was needed and retain or invest it as necessary.

Some Conclusions on Czechoslovakian International Trucking

From this review of the Czechoslovakian scene we can draw out a number of conclusions:

(i)   Czechoslovakian international trucking is not of the scale of the giants of Eastern Europe - Poland and particularly Hungary and Bulgaria - and represents a middle ranking activity by comparison somewhat more significant than the operations of Deutrans in DDR, or Romtrans in Romania.

(ii)   CESMAD has made some attempts to westernise its product and adapt to the needs of operating and competing with western hauliers. It possesses a relatively small number of western trucks; it has an adequate marketing, administrative and organisational structure in place in the West; and it competes for Western European hauls in the open market (albeit with the help of indirect subsidy and low labour costs) with some success.

(iii)   However, it remains relatively backward compared with Hungary and Poland in particular in a number of ways. It still uses East European trucks regularly in the West - Liaz trucks are commonly seen as far as the UK. It has few ancillary services provided for other operations - for example truck maintenance, servicing, repair, fuelling and cleaning - established in Czechoslovakia as hard currency earners. It has made no progress in diversi- fying the company into other products - for example, travel agencies, warehousing, logistics etc - and retains a relatively high proportion of traffic to and from Eastern Europe, particularly to the Soviet Union.

(iv)   Vehicles are still regularly interchanged between the national and international markets reflecting a lack of recognition that different markets with differing client needs, are being catered for.

(v)   Competition is very limited and restricted to a small although growing number of independents and co-operatives. Unlike other East European countries, there is no major competitive element, albeit normally State owned as well, to provide the impetus for adaptation to market forces.

(vi)   There is no evidence of direct subsidy by the State, of CESMAD's activities or that of the operating companies - CSAD. However, undoubt- edly indirect subsidy does exist, particularly through low land and building rents, telephone services and slippage of State aid from the public transport arm.

(vii)   The main advantage that CESMAD has over Western hauliers serving Czechoslovakia, is provided by a cheap labour market, cheap insurance rates and an almost non-existent taxation regime. The latter two items are a form of indirect subsidy as the rates and taxes charged do not meet the costs of the services provided. Hence they represent unfair competiton with the European community conditions of operation for hauliers. Meanwhile, low labour rates are merely a reflection of the State of the economy in Czechoslovakia and does not imply unfair trading.

(viii)   There is no evidence of attempts to penetrate the West European market and take advantage of the changes post-1992 in the European community by establishing truck operating affiliates abroad - unlike Hungary, Poland and Bulgaria.

(ix)   UK government figures for return journeys made by Czechoslovakian hauliers to the UK under bilateral permits for 1981-1988 are:

1981 - 2798	1985 - 2847
1982 - 2647	1986 - 3010
1983 - 2665	1987 - 3969
1984 - 3027	1988 - 4179

Similar figures for UK hauliers to Czechoslovakia are:

1981 - 2457	1985 - 2044
1982 - 2879	1986 - 2204
1983 - 2323	1987 - 2119
1984 - 2213	1988 - 2266

Note the increasing discrepancy reflecting a failure of UK hauliers to match Czechoslo- vakian hauliers in bilateral trade. The reasons for this would appear to centre more on how Czechoslovakian labour rates, and insistence on CIF/FOB export/import contracts by Czechoslovakian foreign trading organizations.

Overall, Czechoslovakian international trucking, and CESMAD/CSAD services in particular, have not benefitted from the long term economic reforms typical of Hungary nor the long term political reforms typical of Poland - and the sudden economic and political changes of 1989/1990 have presented international road freight operators, amongst all other State industries, with immense problems and uncertainties. All this is reflected day to day, in the extensive use of East European manufactured trucks, the lack of a competitive environment, and the failure to take advantage of market position in selling commercial services to others.

Changes undoubtedly will come as Czechoslovakia changes, but it will take time. In the meantime, CESMAD/CSAD continue to offer an East European derived service with limited adaptation to an increasingly discerning market in Czechoslovakia and elsewhere. It seems very unlikely that they will become a major competitor in European trucking after 1992, or as East Europe becomes more market orientated. Instead, unless they adapt quickly, they are more likely to be swamped by the developments in international trucking occurring both in Western Europe and particularly in Hungary, Poland and Bulgaria, in the East.

7 Hungary

General Background

Hungary is a landlocked state located in East-Central Europe at the cross roads of major trade routes both north-south (Baltic-Mediterranean) and East-West (Soviet Union-European Community). As such it has always played a major role in transit traffic by road and rail. It is bordered by Poland, the DDR, Czechoslovakia, Soviet Union and Romania, from the CMEA, and also Yugoslavia and Austria. As a member of CMEA since its foundation, it has been a Socialist controlled country since the late 1940's and as such has displayed an economic structure (including that of the trucking sector) to match. Although State intervention and control has been widespread, in recent years it has declined drastically, perhaps earlier and quicker than elsewhere in Eastern Europe. As such it has faced the problems inherent in this political and economic change earlier than many others, and continues to face severe difficulties to this day.

The Economic Situation in 1990

Economic reform in Hungary has the longest pedigree of any Eastern Bloc state. Politically, free elections for Parliament have been completed during 1990 and Hungary now has been largely transformed from a one party socialist state to one of multi-party democracy. However, this transfer has seriously delayed progress towards economic reform and the proliferation of elected parties makes it more difficult in many ways to continue the economic progress started originally in the 1960's.

At present the Government is faced with the problem of ensuring that the drastic cost to the budget of reducing state subsidies does not seriously undermine its efforts to create a competitive market economy. The uncertain fate of the Government's political and economic policies cannot be ignored and has had a sobering effect on trade. However, despite domestic problems Hungary is clearly determined to press on with its reform programme. Only closer ties with the West can ensure the programme's success and this increasing dependence is bound to boost business relationships, however great the internal economic squeeze. Western economies should be further encouraged by reports that following the decentralisation of foreign trade so many enterprises are now able to trade on their own account that linkage of counter-trade goods between enterprises has become almost impossible. This, coupled with liberalising measures enabling enterprises to import certain products previously only financed by exports of counter-trade goods, has led to a marked drop in the practice of counter-trade generally.

Meanwhile, real growth will remain very modest over the short term at around 0.5%, and inflation at 18% per annum remains a problem. Of more concern, however, is the inability of the authorities to effect a permanent reduction in the current account deficit which deteriorated sharply in the first half of 1989 to $988 million with the likelihood of a $1.4 billion shortfall being registered for the whole year. Most of the deterioration has been due to higher interest payments on the external debt and a sharp fall in net earnings from tourism as increasing numbers of Hungarians travel abroad. The Hungarian authorities project an improvement in the current account deficit in 1990 to around $700 million, but this outturn seems unlikely given that Hungary will require substantial imports of capital goods to facilitate the restructuring of the economy.

Much of the current account shortfall has been covered by borrowing and the external debt is now estimated to be around $19 billion, representing over 67% of GDP. While the debt service ratio has fallen from the 1986 peak of 67%, the current level of 45% implies severe liquidity pressures which are likely to worsen as the country enters a period of higher amortisation payments. Some relief will be forthcoming from the recent decision by the EC to provide Hungary with a five-year ECU 1 billion loan, from further IMF finance and, perhaps, from increased foreign direct investment. In the longer term, however, rescheduling cannot be ruled out.

Overall, Hungary's economic situation is perhaps the worst of all Eastern Europe, excluding Poland. Meanwhile, its political and social reforms are the most advanced and should ensure that the economic reforms necessary can (eventually) be achieved. All this has direct ramifications for the trucking industry reliant, as it always will be, on the success or otherwise of Hungarian industry and agriculture as a whole.

Hungarian Trucking

Currently (1990), there are substantial political, administrative and economic changes taking place in Hungary, which in turn are having noted effects upon ownership, control and style of management of the transport industry, amongst most other industrial and commercial activities.

In terms of Hungarian trucking, once only State ownership existed, which meant that the state, in the form of the appropriate ministry, appointed the industrial leaders, delegated and directed work, controlled prices, presented the level and nature of investment - and much more.

This system of ownership no longer exists and has been dismantled, slowly from 1968, a process that continues to this day. However, its major effects have been really felt only since 1983. The latest stage in the process of reform, affecting all industries, including trucking, centres around the new company legislation introduced late in 1989, which aimed to open up the Hungarian economy to foreign and private investment. For the first time:

(i)   Individual Hungarians may start enterprises, either autonomously or in collaboration with co-operatives or state companies, in any sphere except those specifically reserved for state monopoly - for example, energy. Private companies may employ up to five hundred people.

(ii)   A joint venture with minority foreign shareholdings may be set up without official authorisation.

(iii)   Companies up to 100 percent foreign-owned may be established.

(iv)   The new law, however, also contains a number of clauses that would seem to undermine its main aim. The minimum equity requirement for a limited company (1m forints) and half the capital requirement for a joint stock company (10m forints) must be in cash. Raising such sums would be a major problem for many state enterprises.

The new corporate association law and complementary legislation, including a uniform corporate profit tax law, on the transformation of state enterprises and co-operatives are also expected to provide a further impetus and expansion of private undertakings and joint ventures with foreign partners and it is intended to allow state-owned conglomerates to spin off autonomous corporate units from their plants and subsidiaries.

The new legislation is aimed at improving institutional conditions for small enterprises, helping private entrepreneurs, and opening new possibilities for financial investments that would permit greater capital mobility including private savings.

The law, however, does not resolve the complex problem of ownership rights over state property and the way in which the state as an owner is to be represented in new corporations. All this has obvious ramifications for state owned haulage in Hungary.

State enterprise in trucking remains dominant in the international (and incidentally, national) sector in the form of the major operator Hungarocamion, and its main competitor, Volan. The leading managers in both organisations are still nominated by the state, and there remain controls in the form of direct and indirect taxation, and some financial constraints. However, the opportunities for local initiatives and decision-making have been vastly increased in recent months, including rate-setting, cost allocation, and the allocation of investment, its timing and amount. The new legislation outlined above, is aimed at encouraging this liberalisation process further and faster.

Today (1990), as long as any state enterprise, including those involved in trucking, pays its taxes and other costs (including wages) then it can invest and price services and facilities as it wishes (subject to constraints on hard currency expenditure). The state is left with the residual, but important, control of overall financial policy and taxation levels and direction.

If an enterprise cannot meet its outgoings then it will be declared bankrupt, unlike in the past when the state would have covered all losses. Subsidies have been either dramatically reduced for all industrial/commercial concerns, or in the case of trucking removed altogether, it is claimed. In the case of international road haulage, there has never been any direct subsidy.

However, the State Ministry of Transport, Building and Telecommunications did suggest that in the case of bankruptcy of a major concern (for example, Hungarocamion), then the first option would be one of 're-organisation and restructuring' by the state - suggesting some doubt against the concept of true market freedom and potential bankruptcy.

The basis of all transport policy in Hungary has been redefined in the late 1980's from the socialist principles it once contained so that it now centres upon the principle that all transport should be allocated to the enterprise that is most economical and that operates within the law. This has two ramifications - there should be no protection for state owned enterprises; and no advantages given to private ones over the state. In consequence, the weak should fail and the strong prosper.

One immediately obvious question that arises from this is why should the state retain ownership of the major trucking concerns of Hungarocamion or Volan? The official policy is that state ownership sometimes brings benefits to the country as a whole as profits can be distributed by need through the population. Additionally, privatisation of state industries should only occur if the benefits exceed the drawbacks that commonly occur from losses of economies of scale. Neither appear convincing arguments and reflect the attitudes of state planners, attempting and often failing, to adapt to the new political and economic situation.

Other than state ownership - as in the case of Hungarocamion and Volan, other types of ownership are now growing rapidly in number and significance in the trucking industry:

(i)   Co-operatives, based upon the capital of the owners invested in the trucking company, and not that of the state. Any size co-operative is allowed from one person up to infinity. The distinction of a one person co-operative from independent operator centres on a different legal definition. The same company laws apply to co-operatives as to the state industries - including those relating to bankruptcy.

(ii)   Private ownership - formed again from the private capital of individuals, but legally different from co-operatives. Any size company is permitted up to a maximum of five hundred persons but in the trucking industry the majority are small concerns, commonly only one man and one vehicle. This sector has grown very quickly from 1988.

(iii)   Own account. Industrial transport specifically for the carriage of its own industrial products. This remains a very small sector.

Overall, the policy is one of continued liberalisation with competition between state industries, co-operatives, industries and own account operators, nationally and internationally. However, the question of harmonising the conditions under which they operate (including the issues of licensing and subsidy) remain unresolved.

Entry to the trucking market is subject to quality controls. Trucks can be purchased freely, as long as one has the capital, in unlimited numbers. All operators of all type and size have to meet the following conditions if they are to operate in the international haulage market:

- exhibit good health (drivers only);
- have to be of good repute;
- have to possess sufficient capital;
- need driving experience;
- need driving qualifications (including a special test on international law and regulations);
- have to pass a series of state run psychological tests.

Vehicles are also tested regularly to meet technical requirements internationally applied by the UN and to assess if sufficient land and storage space and maintenance conditions can be met.

In the international trucking sector a licensing system exists, administered by the state. Licences, until 1990, were distributed under a provisional system which is under review. Under this provisional system priority in licences is given as follows:

(i)   Firstly, to long-standing, traditional international hauliers, as a reward for their experience and wide knowledge of markets. This means that Hungarocamion and Volan receive first allocation.

Those companies with contacts with organisations in foreign countries obtain even higher preference as they can more easily secure regular backhauls.

As we shall see later, this gives Hungarocamion the highest priority as they have active partners in Luxemburg, Italy and Austria, plus representatives elsewhere. The justification for this higher priority is that licences are well used as a result of these foreign contacts.

(ii)   Those companies with bigger trucks also get priority, although lower than in group (i), as it ensures that licences are well used. This is to the advantage of Hungarocamion once again who possess the largest of all Hungarian trucks on average.

(iii)   Regular users of licences are next priority - biassing the allocation to those who have obtained licences before - eg Hungarocamion.

(iv)   Own account operators are given a low priority, but higher than:

(v)   Private operators or co-operatives, who receive the lowest priority.

Overall, the Ministry attempts never to reduce the number of licences held by a user, dramatically, even when the new system (outlined on next page) comes into operation. Thus the state allocates the majority of licences to its own industries, and will continue to do this in the foreseeable future.

In late 1990, the new system of licence distribution will be introduced. The basis of this system will be the 'concession', whereby any trucking company granted a concession to trade internationally will be automatically granted a licence. The Ministry will continue to control the system, and the principles of priority allocation of concessions will closely reflect those of the provisional system - hence any change in allocations as a result, will be minimal. This appears to conflict with the professed aims of liberalisation and harmonisation in the trucking market.

Like all other Eastern Bloc countries, the priority in the past in international transport has always been to give preference to rail transport for a number of well documented reasons:

- the potential economies of scale;
- the good infrastructure;
- the priority given to rail development compared to roads since 1945;
- military reasons;
- absence of reliable and economic trucks.

The Hungarian state has recognised in recent years that road transport has much to offer trade and industry and consequently attempts are now being made to reduce the advantages artificially created for rail transport through, in particular, subsidy. However, rail freight is still charged at below actual cost with massive subsidies remaining in all sectors. Although there are now no requirements for any industry (state or private) to use the rail network, whilst these subsidies remain, there will continue to be an artificially large market for rail distribution.

As part of the process of harmonising transport conditions, there are substantial plans in Hungary to develop the road network, and in particular, the construction of a new motorway between Budapest and Wein. Funds to pay for this development are severely limited by economic problems, but have been relieved by finance available through the Hungary-Austria Expo project. A new ring road around Budapest is also planned and partially constructed but completion will be a very slow process.

Hard currency issues remain dominant in the life of Hungarian industry including the international trucking sector where hard currency can be earned relatively easily. Convertibility of the forint is not likely until at least 1992, although government plans (lacking in detail) to achieve it by then, do exist.

It is openly admitted that the main reason behind Hungarocamion's formation in 1966 was to earn hard currency. Previously all international goods movements to the West were conducted by rail or used the partner country's road services. By rail, only that part of the journey in Hungary would be paid for in forints with the rest payable in hard currency. By road, all payments were in hard currency.

Consequently, international road haulage by Hungarian operators saves hard currency as expenses can be partly paid for in forints (eg wages, some fuel, insurance etc), and if carrying for Western industry, actually earns hard currency for the company and state. It is for these reasons that Hungary, like all the Eastern Bloc countries, have traditionally exported CIF, and imported FOB - hence controlling the transport operation in both directions, saving and earning hard currency as a result.

Today, Hungarian international trucks still earn hard currency and forints - depending on the industry paying the cost of transport. The major part are the former currencies, by design.

Each international trucking company, state owned or otherwise, by law, must pay all earnings into the State Bank. Two accounts are then created:

- a forint account;
- a hard currency account.

The forint account is simple. Forints earned by international trucking from Hungarian industries are paid into an account from which the trucking company can draw as it wishes to pay wages, bills, insurance and so on. There are no state controls on its usage - apart from normal business and commercial law.

The hard currency account is more complex. All hard currency by law must be returned to the state. It thus must pass through a hard currency account whereby 40% can be retained by the trucking company in its original form. However, it can only be spent on authorised items, agreed by the state. The remaining 60% has to be converted to forints and the hard currency goes to the state for its use. The converted forints then are transferred to the forint account for use as the trucking company wishes.

Clearly such a system has drawbacks for international trucking companies - in particular, they are far from free in what they can do and spend, and there is only a limited incentive to earn more hard currency, since the main part they never see. However, it is a well-known and understood system which is predictable. The state interferes little in other ways and the trucking companies do keep all the profits they make, subject to the compulsory conversion rules. Taxation of profits is applied by the state.

Overall, therefore, Hungary is moving towards a free international trucking economy. The future will see moves towards more privatisation, currency conversion and reduced subsidy but there are considerable resistances to be overcome at all levels, political, organisational and economic, before they can be achieved. We will now go on to examine three examples of international trucking in Hungary in some detail, to assess the progress made and the likelihood of success in the light of the changes taking place.

Hungarocamion

Hungarocamion was formed on 1 January 1966 with the basic aim of providing reliable and efficient international road transport for both Hungarian and foreign customers. At the time of its foundation the company possessed only 357 small capacity vehicles (mainly Skoda, Csepel and Sauer makes) of which 89% were tilt units, 10% refrigerated and 1% specials. In the first year of operation, Hungarocamion vehicles performed 21m km and achieved 185m tonne/km. By the late 1980's this had increased to 134m km and 1582 m tonne/km.

In 1990, the Hungarocamion company structure consisted of a large number of subsidiary units operating under the umbrella of the main holding company. The five main branches are shipping management, technical services, financial services, personnel and social services, and business policy and marketing. Within each of these branches there are a number of specialised groups.

Hungarocamion has always been, and remains, state owned and until recently was the only Hungarian road haulier operating internationally. Since the 1970's, some competition has developed, and as we shall see later, this competition has grown rapidly in the last two or three years. It now not only operates international haulage, but also acts as a forwarder; maintains, repairs and services its own and other fleets; and provides a variety of financial, legal and business services both for itself and others.

Despite remaining under state ownership, it is now legally possible for Hungarocamion to go bankrupt in the same way as a West European haulier. No direct subsidies are provided for any of its functions, although there is little doubt that indirect subsidy (in the form of cheap or non existent rents, cheap loans, subsidised fuel etc) has existed and may continue to do so. It is actively denied by senior management.

Privatisation is not planned for the near future although as a relatively prosperous and modern company, Hungarocamion must be a prime target and a buyer (or buyers) could be found easily. Senior management at Hungarocamion felt that privatisation was unlikely soon for a number of reasons, including:

- Hungarocamion does not need the extra capital that privatisation usually brings as its hard currency earnings were so large.

- It was efficiently managed and consequently privatisation would bring few benefits.

- Although the state did need the income from privatisation, a single sale of a high hard currency earner would provide no long-term solution to this problem.

Additionally, a recent World Bank loan would provide all the additional capital needed in the short and middle term.

Hungarocamion has a long history of operating throughout West Europe and the Middle East and as a result has a well established network of representatives in many other countries. Some two hundred agents are maintained in foreign countries, plus sixteen of their own employees in sixteen countries across Europe and the Near and Middle East.

As part of the process of company development and increasing access to Western Europe and other diversified markets, Hungarocamion has developed a number of affiliate companies. They include three trucking companies in Western Europe:

- Eurocar of Trieste (Italy) - 40 refrigerated vehicles;
- Hungarolux of Luxembourg - 60 tilt trailers and tractors;
- Peklar of Wein (Austria) - 20 mixed vehicles.

These three companies provide direct access to the European Community and other West European markets both before, and significantly after 1992, including:

- greater access to permits;
- provide facilities for Hungarian vehicles in the West;
- access to backhauls;
- easier repatriation of hard currency profits;
- access to the post 1992 Single European Market.

Each of these companies is run on a commercial basis with services provided for affiliate companies (eg Hungarocamion) and others at profit-making rates and in local (hard) currency.

Other companies set up by Hungarocamion outside of direct international trucking include:

- Eurogate Ltd - forwarding agents based in Budapest and London;
- a driver centre just outside Budapest providing food, wash facilities, accommodation etc, 60% owned by Hungarocamion;
- a truck racing company, based in Budapest and used for marketing purposes;
- Transpack, a Hungarian packaging company jointly owned with Volan;
- a travel agency in Budapest;
- a heavy transport company in Budapest;
- a limited groupage and warehousing company based in Budapest.

During 1990 it is anticipated that Timesped will be established as a joint venture with western involvement, providing full logistics facilities within Hungary.

Hungarocamion also operate ten border crossing offices (see Table 11) which not only expedite Hungarocamion shipments but also provide services at cost, to other vehicles, Hungarian and foreign, including permit issue, customs services, technical assistance and other requirements.

The main source of trade for Hungarocamion remains the state owned and operated Trading Companies who act as agents between the transport operator (eg MAV - state rail; Hungarocamion and Malev - state airline), the exporters and the importers. Over the years Hungarocamion has developed close relationships with these companies which will continue as they are privatised in the coming months.

The second source of trade is through forwarding agents, privately owned and operated who have developed in large numbers since 1988. Later we shall examine the operation of one of these agents, Deltasped, in some detail.

Thirdly, a major source is now directly, through industrial or agricultural concerns who export or import using a foreign trade licence granted by the state. These licences, comparatively new on the scene, are becoming more widely available as time passes. The only condition in most industries is that the company concerned must have on its staff someone with experience in foreign trade negotiations.

Between 60 and 70% of Hungarocamion loads are imports or more commonly exports to and from Hungarian companies. The remainder is cross-trade traffic. Hungarocamion claim that 90% of all Hungarian international road traffic was carried by them; 7-8% by their main competitor Volan; and 2-3% by a large number of independents and co-operatives. This latter group, it was accepted, was expanding rapidly, but from a very small base.

Cross-trading remains a significant part of Hungarocamion's activities, but it is declining in size. The main market is now between Western Europe (particularly Italy, France, Belgium, West Germany and the UK) and Poland or the Soviet Union.

The main market for all Hungarocamion traffic is Western Europe, and this market continues to expand as a relative and absolute proportion of total traffic carried. Destinations served reflect the trading patterns of Hungary as a whole - thus 40% of all freight carried by Hungarocamion is destined for West Germany (although this includes traffic for Hamburg and onward transport to the USA, Japan, Canada etc), with Austria and Italy being the other main destinations and sources of traffic. Elsewhere

TABLE 11 : HUNGAROCAMION BORDER OFFICES, 1990

COUNTRY	LOCATION	HOURS	SERVICES
A	Mosonmagyarovar	Non-stop	All offices:
Cs	Rajka	Non-stop	Permit issue; route permits
A	Hegyeshalom	Non-stop	heavy vehicles; customs
A	Sopron	M-F Non-stop Sat 0600-1600 Sun 0600-2200	guarantees; customs documentation; technical
Yu	Letenye	Non-stop	assistance.
Yu	Roszke	Non-stop	
R	Nagylak	Non-stop	
Su	Zahony	Daily 0700-2200	
Cs	Vamosszabad	Non-stop	
A	Szentgotthard	M-F 0630-2200 Sat 0630-1500 Sun Closed	

Source : Hungarocamion

in Western Europe, significant if small quantities of traffic originate and are destined for the UK, Spain, Netherlands, France, Belgium and Scandinavia. Other destinations in West Europe were less frequently served and included Eire, Portugal and Switzerland. (Table 12 gives more details of regular groupage facilities available)

As the major provider of international road freight services to Western Europe from Hungary, Hungarocamion benefits from processing a large number of permanent licences for international road transport - far in excess of those provided to any other operator. This is an issue of continuous contention in terms of the equity of licence distribution within Hungary and the supposedly liberal and harmonised market that is being created.

Near and Middle East traffic has declined drastically in recent years and groupage traffic is now restricted to a trip to Kuwait every ten days, plus occasional, irregular trips to Iran and Iraq depending on demand. In 1984/1985, nearly 5,000 return journeys a year were being made by Hungarocamion trucks to these markets. In 1990, it will be between sixty and eighty (including Kuwaiti groupage). The reasons for the decline are well documented and have affected all other Eastern (and Western) European hauliers. They include the effects of the Iran-Iraq war and the growth of competition particularly from Turkish hauliers. Other than groupage to Iran, Iraq and Kuwait, there remain only occasional trips to Turkey and the Lebanon.

In Eastern Europe, the main method of controlling international road haulage is the multi-lateral agreement between the Eastern Bloc countries. It stipulates that all commodities must be sold to the sellers county border,and then taken on from there under a new order - involving therefore, at least two contracts and sets of paperwork for each movement.

Meanwhile, rail transport is heavily subsidised and until recently given priority through direct traffic diversion in Hungary (and elsewhere). Consequently the East European international road haulage market is relatively small and largely unprofitable. It also brings in no hard currency (until January 1991 when all CMEA intra-payments will have to be in hard currencies).

Hungary's main East European trading partner is the Soviet Union, but here there are even greater problems in acquiring traffic at a profitable

TABLE 12 : HUNGAROCAMION GROUPAGE SERVICES, 1990

DESTINATION	REGULAR DEPARTURES A WEEK	RUNNING TIME
Bielefeld (D)	2	3
London (UK)	2	4
Bradford (UK)	2	4
Strasbourg (D)	1	3
Lyon (F)	1	3
Paris (F)	1	3
Thessaloniki (GR)	1	2.5
Athens (GR)	1	3
Munich (D)	3	2
Wuppertal (D)	2	3
Frankfurt (D)	2	3
Wien (A)	2	1
Milan (I)	1	3
Bologna (I)	Occasionally	3
Prato (I)	Occasionally	3
Kuwait (Kuwait)	Every 10 days	10
Malmo (S)	2	3
Kopenhagen (DK)	1	3
Montzen (CH)	1	3
Basel (CH)	1	3
Buchs/Feldkirch (CH)	1	2
Heurne (NL)	2	3
Rotterdam (NL)	2	3
Amsterdam (NL)	2	3

DESTINATION	REGULAR DEPARTURES A WEEK	RUNNING TIME
Helsinki (SF)	2	4
Lisbon/Porto (P)	2	10
	(via Wuppertal)	
Hamburg (D)	2	3
Barcelona (E)	3	10
	(via Munich)	
Tehran (Iran)	Occasionally	10
Baghdad (Iraq)	Occasionally	10

Source : Hungarocamion

rate. Ninety percent of all goods between Hungary and the USSR move by rail. Nine percent move by Soviet trucks, leaving only 1% for air, pipeline, sea/river and Hungarian international trucking and cross-traders. Of this 1%, three quarters of Hungarian international trucking is carried by Volan and Hungarocamion only one quarter. Volan acquire this bigger share, despite being a much smaller operation than Hungarocamion, by offering very low rates, applying low standards of speed, reliability and quality of service, and using Eastern European trucks. Almost no USSR backhauls are available, whilst Hungary to USSR backhauls are available to USSR hauliers. Consequently, Hungarocamion concentrates on Western European traffic.

As with most international trucking, Hungarocamion relies on <u>backhauls</u> to produce profits, and claim that on Western European runs, 80% of returning journeys acquire a load. The main source of these backhauls are the representatives and agents scattered around West Europe and the Near and Middle East. Their main task is to acquire backhauls and also to obtain industrial information on orders about to be made. The agent then enquires about transport needs related to these orders thus hopefully acquiring the load for Hungarocamion. Without maintaining this backhaul level, Hungarocamion could not make a profit.

The present vehicle fleet of Hungarocamion consists of 1600 tractor and trailer units manufactured by Raba/Man, Mercedes, Renault, Volvo and Scania, and a diversity of trailers suited to the variety of markets that exist - Raba, Budamobil, Kassbohrer, Blumhardt-Crane, Lamberet, Fruehauf, Unicar etc. About 1100 trailers are normal tilts, another 160 are specialist vehicles including container chassis, clothes carriers, furniture carriers, liquid and granulate tankers, pneumatic protected carriers for sensitive equipment, flower carriers and livestock trailers. The remainder of the fleet, some 340 trucks are refrigerated vehicles, a declining number and proportion of the total fleet. This decline is due to four reasons:

-         a decline in food imports and exports;
-         backhauls are difficult to obtain for such specialised vehicles in such a peaked market;
-         profit levels are low;
-         vehicles are expensive.

Hungary still exports considerable quantities of fruit and vegetables needing refrigerated vehicles, especially in March and October. During these two months, 340 vehicles is insufficient but backhauls are still very difficult to obtain. In winter, the vehicles are in demand for the import of citrus fruits and bananas from the Near East and the ports of Northern Europe, but there are no exports to fill the vehicles in the other direction. Consequently, severe peaking occurs and profits are difficult to maintain. Hence, the relative and absolute decline in this sector as Hungarocamion becomes more commercially minded and less a state department.

The vast majority of West European services are provided using West European vehicles or Raba trucks, produced in Gyor, Hungary, but to a relatively modern Man design. Other East European trucks (eg Liaz and older Raba vehicles) are reserved for East European international journeys, or the Hungarian portion of Western trips. The widely known reasons are behind this choice of vehicle allocation - costs of maintenance; costs of operation; marketing reasons; quality of service etc.

Trucks are serviced in two main depots around Budapest, one specialising in Mercedes, Renault and Volvo, the other in Scania and Ford/Iveco. Minor repairs and servicing is carried out at local depots either in Budapest or around Hungary. When Western vehicles become too old for Hungarocamion use, normally after about seven years, then they are either sold to independent/co-operative users for the international or national market; or are transferred to the national fleet for local usage or transport within East Europe. Hungarocamion has established a separate company specifically for the marketing and distribution of second-hand East and West European vehicles of which many were in evidence (some 150-200) now out of use, at the Budapest main depot.

Hungarocamion drivers are paid wages that reflect the cheaper costs of living in Hungary (average wages are about $130 per month and hence are relatively low compared with Western Europe), but also the needs and problems of travelling in the West for extensive periods. The basic rule is that drivers are paid through an incentive scheme whereby wages are related to mileage covered and their ability to keep to a standard average speed of 15 kph (including rest periods). If this average speed is bettered, then incentives are paid at a rate of 33% above the norm in terms of hard currency allowance. However, for safety reasons, such allowances are limited to a maximum of 96DM per day. Drivers are not entirely happy with this arrangement as a really quick journey will not be adequately rewarded due to the state limit on incentives. The result is that drivers commonly travel as fast as possible on a return trip, but may wait in Austria for a day or more to claim extra days' allowances, and still receive a maximum speed bonus.

Insurance cover is related to the Green Card scheme and is provided for third party cover only and vehicle contents. Rates in Hungary are very low for all European destinations, but high for the Near and Middle East, adding to the problems of this market.

No vehicle road tax is payable in Hungary as it is included within the price of fuel. In March 1990 the price of a litre of diesel was 17ft (about 17p), 30% higher than December 1989, 10ft of which is duty. Direct comparison with Western European fuel prices reveals the low price of fuel in Hungary, which is made Moreso since it includes vehicle taxation which is normally charged additionally in the West. However, there are many regulations that control the import of fuel into many West European countries and as a result, cheap Eastern European imports of fuel are not possible on a large scale. Consequently, the cost advantage of Hungarian fuel to Hungarian operators is limited by this. At the same time, Western hauliers in Hungary can only purchase diesel for hard currency, at punitive rates of exchange.

Rate fixing is a decision totally and solely for Hungarocamion. There is no state interference on pricing now, and it was limited in the past. Discounts on standard prices are regularly available on imports aimed at attracting backhauls and, it is claimed, to compete with Western hauliers. Partly due to the nature of the Hungarian market (imports are small in size, weight and yet high in value; exports are larger in size and weight and lower in value), there are approximately five loads of exports to every one of imports. Overall, Hungary's foreign trade balance is positive with the West in value, and very positive in terms of weight and volume.

Discounts are also available on regular and long-term orders and those which are irregular, but substantial in size. Generally speaking, most rates are negotiated around a set standard. Regular customers get guarantees of vehicle space during busy periods. Agents are used to book ferry crossings to Scandinavia, UK and Eire combining vehicle shipments from the Eastern Bloc as a whole to produce economies of scale and advantages in price negotiations.

Overall, Hungarocamion give every impression of a well managed, modern company ready for the changes occurring in East Europe, and their exposure to market forces. There has undoubtedly been state subsidy in the past and indirectly there may well remain today in the form of low rents, cargo direction, cheap loans and so on. The vehicle fleet is modern, well maintained and presented. Hungarocamion have a strong and well established marketing and fleet and cargo management structure in the West and the company appears poised to prosper and develop in the new economic environment. Already the company is divided into separate profit centres, each charging realistic commercial rates (given Hungary's low labour rates) for services provided to each other and to outsiders. Bankruptcy threatens if they fail - although this has yet to happen. Competition is small but growing quickly and acting as a market stimulus.

Hungarocamion represents perhaps the most advanced and well structured road haulage company in the Eastern Bloc requiring little more than advice and some training of management to produce a company that can compete on a commercial basis throughout Europe.

Volan

The majority of material in this section was derived from discussions with management at the Kisalfold Branch of Volan, located at Gyor in North-West Hungary.

Each county administrative region in Hungary has a Volan company to provide freight transport, once only within that county. Volan was then an effective state monopoly of road freight, nationally. In recent years, Volan has diversified so that almost every branch now provides services intra and inter county, and internationally. Since 1988 each Volan company has been legally separate from one another and operated as a profit centre in itself. However, a common Volan council formed of representatives from each of the Volan companies, exists as an advisory and policy body located in Budapest. This umbrella organisation distributes licences, provides common marketing facilities, is a forum for discussion of problems and provides common representation abroad. It has no power over the individual operating companies and receives very limited funding from them.

Prior to this arrangement, the Volan companies were all dependent on one another and the rich ones cross- subsidised the poor (and the efficient, the inefficient). Now that cross-subsidy is no longer possible, each company has to survive alone, and many have turned to international transport to provide extra income. Gradually, each of the Volan companies have now entered the international market.

All Volan companies remain a hundred percent state owned. In each county there is normally a central administrative point adjoining a main maintenance and servicing centre. Throughout each county there is also a number of local garaging points where minor maintenance can be carried out. Some would be responsible for international vehicles. Thus in the Kisalfold county:

Main centre   - Gyor   - 66 international and
                                 national trucks;
Local centres - Csorna   - 3 international trucks;
              - Kapovar   - national only;
              - Beled   - 16 international trucks;
              - Sopron   - national only;
              - Moronmagyar   - national only.

Each local centre operates national vehicles and provides maintenance, cleaning, fueling, servicing and repair facilities for its own vehicles and others (including other companies) at commercial cost. The distribution and number of international vehicles is related to the distribution of customers in the local market.

Volan had experimented with international trucking to a limited extent, from 1970, but it was restricted to Eastern Europe and controlled by the state, centrally. From 1988 expansion into the Western European market has taken place - particularly Scandinavia, Turkey, Greece, Italy, West Germany, Austria, Yugoslavia and the Netherlands. Very occasionally services are provided to France, the UK, Switzerland and Belgium. No services are provided to the Near and Middle East.

Volan's fleet consists mainly of Raba trucks - Hungarian manufactured from a Man design. Some Czechoslovakian made Liaz (Skoda) trucks are used for wholly East European journeys. Very few Western made trucks are operated - for example, Kisalfold had a limited number of leased Iveco Fords. This is not because Eastern European trucks are preferred, but that hard currency earnings are yet to reach sufficient levels to finance Western vehicle purchase or leasing. It is widely agreed in the Volan organisation that for marketing, operational and economic reasons, Western vehicles are preferable.

The main Volan market comes from direct contact with industrial and agricultural groups, usually local to the Volan county concerned, thus limiting dead mileage. There is no legal reason why contracts from all over Hungary cannot be agreed - in fact the Gyor based Volan company did have one such contract in Pecs in the south of the county and another in Miskolc, in the far East.

The international fleet is kept separately from the national fleet as it is newer, in better condition and limited to Raba, Liaz and a few western vehicles. The average age of the international fleet is five to eight years, but few are newer than three years, and some are up to fifteen years old.

Backhauls are of great significance to Volan, who plan and achieve a 70-75% level of return loads. Agents or representatives are maintained in all the countries which are major markets for Hungarian goods. Commonly they are expatriate Hungarians who are paid in hard currency by the central Volan organisation to avoid duplication of representation and to achieve economies of scale. It was admitted that even Hungarocamion contacts abroad are used to find backhauls (and vice versa).

Pricing is based upon cost plus profit as there are no direct subsidies for freight transport either national or international in Hungary. However, one needs to question whether the subsidies openly paid to local Volan public transport occasionally or regularly 'slip' into the international road freight sector, for example through the use of the same garaging and maintenance facilities, same staff etc.

The price structure for international transport is based around kilometrage operated and varies according to the countries traversed to reflect taxes, fuel costs and so on. Each company operation charges their own rates. Routing of international services is adjusted to avoid the more costly countries (for example Austria). Kisalfold Volan estimate that a 20 tonne laden weight, full truck costs to operate:

In Hungary	- 50ft a km	)	not allowing
International average	- 80-100ft a km	)	for
Austria	- 120-130ft a km	)	any backhaul

Wages are paid by the kilometre and by time. Whilst abroad in the West drivers are paid in local (hard) currency as a daily allowance. A standard time and distance is calculated for each destination and any excess is not paid unless a driver can prove extenuating circumstances. If the journey is completed in less time or distance than the driver keeps the excess allowance, plus (as we saw earlier) he receives a limited bonus. If driving with a backhaul, then extra allowances are paid, providing an incentive to drivers to contact representatives abroad and to acquire return loads.

Volan have to meet the same regulations that are imposed on all international freight drivers, including those of Hungarocamion, independents and co-operatives:

- each driver must attend a special course to learn foreign driving rules, basic international legislation and some basic foreign languages;
- each driver must have three years minimum driving experience of heavy freight vehicles;
- they must be at least twenty one;
- they must pass a series of psychological tests to assess driving suitability.

Volan believe the distribution of international operating licences to be unfair. The growth of co-operatives and independents and the power of Hungarocamion in licence distribution has resulted in Volan receiving less licences than they need. The process of distribution, although largely public remains open to many criticisms from almost all those involved.

Volan has not diversified beyond international transport at the moment and remains outside of international warehousing or logistics - although it is involved in the former on a national basis. The only real move so far away from haulage is a part share with Hungarocamion in Transpack - a packaging company.

Privatisation of Volan is not likely soon, although the bankruptcy laws do apply now. Currently, the main changes taking place are aimed at splitting the Volan companies up into ever smaller units to increase the element of competition.

Overall, Volan is the main competitor to Hungarocamion in the international road freight sector, but are small by comparison, limited to restricted markets and have a small market share. Quality of operations, particularly vehicle type and age is generally inferior, whilst company management is more akin to the East Europe of old. It is unlikely whether Volan can survive Western competition, or exposure to a free market in the international sector. However, partially protected as they are now, they provide limited competition to Hungarocamion and thus help to encourage a more efficient road haulage sector overall.

Volan provides an interesting example of a state owned company attempting to adapt to the demands of the new market. Unlike Hungarocamion it has not benefitted from large hard currency earnings over many years and this may prove to be a notable problem for it in the short and long term, in the international sector.

Deltasped

The final case study from Hungary relates to a privately owned freight forwarding company established in Budapest, who have dealings with Hungarocamion, Volan and the independent/co-operative international road transport sector. It thus provides a relatively independent view of the international road haulage market in 1990.

Deltasped is an independent company for forwarding freight anywhere in the world. Its share capital is divided into three groups:

- one third belongs to a Hungarian co-operative haulier;
- one third belongs to Transforwarding, a Dutch haulier based in Rotterdam;
- one third belongs to individuals in Budapest who formed the companies. These eight individuals all work within the company.

One major advantage of this shared ownership is that the Hungarian haulier owns thirty relatively new Renault trucks. However, as the forwarder does not own these trucks they are commonly used for other purposes; but priority use is given when possible, to Deltasped needs. Deltasped have no ambitions to acquire their own trucks as it is better to specialise in what they know and in which they have greatest experience - forwarding.

Deltasped has two offices - one in central Budapest and one based at the Hungarian road freight operator. Demand for transport by Deltasped is between 80 and 100 trucks daily and consequently far more than is available from the Hungarian co-operative. The surplus of vehicles is hired with drivers from private independents, other co-operatives and even Volan and Hungarocamion. The result is Deltasped's co-operative has a constant flow of almost guaranteed work, whilst peeks are covered by other operators, particularly the private sector.

A network of agents and representatives are maintained throughout Europe to obtain backhauls - and it was claimed that a 95% level of return loads was achieved. These return loads were usually negotiated whilst a vehicle was away, travelling on an export run. Drivers are requested to telephone the local agent and Deltasped headquarters in Budapest to establish whether a load is available. Communications by fax are used to arrange backhaul organisation.

Deltasped survive through good personal contacts within a large variety of industries, other transport and forwarding companies and overseas agents. They do not possess good contacts with the state owned FTO's, unlike Hungarocamion and Volan - and may benefit from this in the future as the latter are run down and the opportunity is given to private industry to develop and expand its overseas operating and contacts.

Deltasped is a company that has developed under the new regime. It was established on 1 October 1989 and already has amassed enough capital soon to open a warehouse and packaging centre, and with plans for an import/export business of office furniture. Liberalisation was felt to have worked for them as a forwarding and haulage business. Deltasped has benefitted particularly through its contacts with the West in the form of Transforwarding in the Netherlands, who not only find backhauls for Hungarian vehicles but also under new Hungarian taxation laws provide an opportunity to pay a lower rate of taxation in Hungary. It also provides a means of utilising hard currency without having to involve the Hungarian state authorities. For example, for every 100DM earned, normally 60% would have to be exchanged for Hungarian forints (under state law) and the remainder could be kept and used as Deutsch Marks. But as Transforwarding own a third share of the company 33.3DM can be repatriated to the Netherlands without any penalty, leaving only 66.6DM to suffer the 60% forint penalty. The benefits of a Western connection are clear.

Overall, Deltasped gave an impression of success, created by hard work and the benefit of liberalisation from the old state ideas and constraints. They provide consistent work for the private sector, both independent and co-operative hauliers and even some work for the state owned haulage sector - Hungarocamion and Volan. Certainly it seems likely that private forwarders and hauliers will continue to grow and provide competition to the established marker leaders. However, one should not underestimate the market lead held by Hungarocamion and the fact that it will be retained for many years to come.

Conclusions

A number of conclusions can be drawn from this review of the Hungarian international haulage sector:

(i)   The relatively modern condition of the state owned Hungarocamion vehicle fleet and its adoption of a relatively efficient marketing and organisational structure.

(ii)   The rather less modern and less efficient organisation of the main competitor, Volan, surviving upon business which Hungarocamion does not wish to take on in markets where the profit margin is small and irregular.

(iii)   The clear dominance of Hungarocamion in terms of fleet size, technical facilities, market share, marketing organisation, overseas representation, quality of service and administrative back-up.

(iv)   The growth of the private sector, both independents and co-operatives, in competition with the state owned grants. However, this growth is from a very small base and hence this sector remains relatively small.

(v)   The failure to privatise any part of the state haulage groups at the moment, and the absence of any clear-cut plans, at the moment, to do so. This is surprising given the relatively strong economic condition of Hungarocamion in particular.

(vi)   The dominance of Western traffic in this market sector, based on hard currency need, historical precedence and trends within the market place.

(vii)   The development of East European and other West European based affiliate companies to ensure easy access to the European Community market post 1992.

(viii) The problems that face the Hungarian economy in the short term are immense with a vast foreign debt and an unconvertible currency. Economic revision may spell disaster for international hauliers, particularly the smaller independents and co-operatives who receive no indirect subsidies and have little in financial reserve.

(ix)   Low labour, insurance and taxation costs for all Hungarian international hauliers and the probability of continued indirect subsidy for Hungarocamion and Volan even though any direct subsidy that might have once existed, has now been removed.

(x)   There is no real evidence at Hungarocamion or Volan of state intervention in pricing, load direction or vehicle operations, nor of interference in management organisation or middle and low ranking appointments. However, senior management is still chosen by the state. Each haulage company, State or privately owned, will now go bankrupt if circumstances dictate. However, the likelihood of the larger, state owned companies suffering this fate seems rather less than that of the smaller independents and co-operatives.

8 Poland

General Background

Poland is a medium sized country of 312,683 km, situated in Eastern Central Europe. It belonged to the socialised bloc and remains, currently (1990), a member of CMEA, surrounded by other CMEA members - the USSR, DDR and Czechoslovakia. In area and population, it is the seventh state of Europe.

Poland is inhabited by thirty six million people at a density of 113 persons per square mile. Fifty nine percent of the population is urban based in cities relatively evenly distributed throughout the country. Thirty five cities have a population of more than 100,000 inhabitants, five over 500,000. The two largest districts are Upper Silesia in the south, dominantly industrial (with three million inhabitants) and Warsaw, in the east central area, with two million.

The Polish economy is mixed industrial and agricultural. Developing since the Second World War has been a mix of heavy industry, including mining, metallurgy, engineering and chemicals. Coal is a very significant industry (fourth in the world) as is lignite, copper, sulphur and iron and steel.

Agriculture is characterised by a private farming section of small units. Only 20% of Polish agriculture is state owned. Large quantities of potatoes, rye, milk, sugar beet and oats are produced, but insufficient in most cases to cope with internal demand.

The Polish economy is rather more difficult to summarise as it is characterised by highly fluctuating demand led inflation until mid 1990, indebtedness mainly to the West, and heavy state subsidies. Inflation, in particular, has been a major cause of concern to all organisations within Poland, and has been subject to a number of policies aimed at its control and reduction. In particular, these have included:

(i)   Cutting industrial/commercial/government costs by reducing the number employed, creating unemployment for the first time for fifty years. This has affected the trucking industry in two ways - firstly by reducing the numbers employed by the state - and secondly by encouraging the newly unemployed into private trucking enterprises as a new form of employment. Understandably, many of the latter ultimately will fail.

(ii)   An increase in interest rates to curb the demand for loans, again affecting the trucking industry by making the financing of trucks by both private and state companies more expensive.

(iii)   Severely increased state budget discipline resulting in massively reduced subsidy, including those to the trucking industry.

All three measures require a reduction in state subsidy to all sectors, including that of trucking. The result has, and will continue to be a reduction in inflation from a peak of 180% in January 1990 alone, to 75% in February, 10% in March and 3% in April, but a concomitant massive increase in unemployment and a reduction of around 20% in production, affecting amongst other things, the demand for trucking services.

The stabilization of the exchange rate at 9,500 zloty to the US$ in January 1990 has produced a level of economic stability unknown in recent years, and will remain fixed until at least the end of 1990. However, in turn, this has made purchase of Western goods and services considerably more expensive. This will make international trucking more dominated by Polish hauliers, but will also place financial pressures on those same hauliers in attempting to renew Western equipment.

This situation is made all the more complex by an ever changing political and economic situation which in the last two years has seen the demise of socialism, free elections and moves towards privatisation of industry and a convertible national currency (zloty). In broadest terms Poland is attempting to move as quickly as possible, and quicker than any other East European country, towards a totally liberalised market economy, from one dominated by state planning. The haulage sector within Poland is typical of these moves, and as we go on we shall see how changes within the Polish economic/political/legal systems are affecting international and national haulage operations.

Haulage Prior to 1989

To understand the current economic and organisational chaos we need to examine the situation prior to the massive economic and political changes that have taken place.

Until 1989, virtually all transport of freight and passengers in Poland was state controlled and based upon four enterprises all controlled by the then Ministry of Transport and Communications.

(a)   Public Trucking

(i)   Domestic Market This was organised regionally through the PKS set of enterprises, one for each of the seventeen administrative areas. Central organisation came from Warsaw. All public goods distribution was controlled through PKS including distribution to retail outlets from manufacturing plants and warehouses. Main movements of materials and goods between region were made by rail to depots located in each region from which local delivery by road was organised. Within each region a number of operating depots would exist with lorries strictly allocated to each. Until 1985, lorries were not normally moved between operating depots or regions with consequential inefficiencies occurring as a result.

(ii)   International Market International goods transport by road was organised by a state owned near monopoly - PEKAES which was operated as an arm of the PKS domestic transport service.

132

Exporters and importers were required to use PEKAES if road transport had to be used for transport purposes. The vast majority of international goods, however, were directed towards the rail and sea sector.

(b)   Individual Transport

Transport by road organised for a particular economic activity - for example, the coal, building or iron and steel industries. The main activities were the carriage of personnel to and from employment; materials and components for the industry concerned; and distribution of finished products locally.

(c)   Factory Transport

Vehicles owned by manufacturing concerns to distribute finished products to retail outlets. This was a very small sector.

(d)   Private Enterprise Trucking

Until 1989 this was a small sector consisting of individual operators normally with one vehicle. Domestic distribution of goods was the main trade filling in gaps when state hauliers were unavailable. The scale of activity was never known accurately but was felt to be larger than officially recognised.

A system of licensing existed until 1987 whereby international road transit was compelled to use PEKAES - unless reasons could be shown otherwise. (For example, PEKAES had no suitable vehicles available, and therefore a Western haulier or another East European haulier would be used). Meanwhile domestic road haulage was allowed only for distances up to 50km from the local region. For any greater distances a special permit was required for each trip - a process that was both bureaucratic and slow. Transport by both factory and industry vehicles was restricted to the industries concerned.

International permits were also used between East European countries, dividing traffic between the state hauliers concerned. This system remains with decisions about the number of permits made at annual meetings.

Between 1987 and 1989 substantial changes were made in the organisation of road freight transport in Poland.

(i) The licensing system was revoked allowing all groups to operate in all markets, national and international, any distance they wished. Vehicles can now be transferred, loaned or hired between sectors.

(ii) PEKAES is now no longer entirely state owned and has been reconstituted as a joint stock company, 51% owned by the State and 49% by a variety of other groups (including other state companies, some private companies and some non- Polish groups). The latter have close economic links with Poland.

(iii) A new business act of 1 November 1988 encouraged and allowed wide use of private haulage including the introduction of an agency system with the possibility of self-employed drivers using state-owned vehicles, paid in terms of incentives - ie more journeys, more income.

(iv) The Ministry of transport and Marine Economy has replaced the old Ministry of Transport and Communications and now includes all transport and related activities. The organisational structure in relation to trucking is now one of:

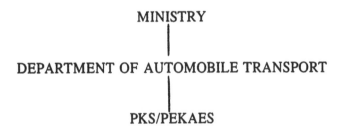

MINISTRY

|

DEPARTMENT OF AUTOMOBILE TRANSPORT

|

PKS/PEKAES

Polish government policy is now one of overt encouragement of privatisation in road haulage both domestic and international, particularly through the agency system and that of selling state companies to private industry - either Polish or otherwise. The latter approach involves selling companies, their assets and debts, and may result in redundancies and certainly the loss of subsidy.

International Trucking Post 1987

Since 1987, a number of alternative competitors to PEKAES have developed, encouraged by the state to provide a semblance of a competitive market.

(i)   PKS regional operators have established 'Autotransport' to operate internationally in competition with PEKAES. As it has emerged from PKS it remains State owned and is administered by the same part of the Ministry that has residual responsibility for PEKAES. It thus provides state competition to a state operator but does produce economies of scale for domestic operators with under-used vehicles. It owns a number of its own specialised international vehicles, and has to pay commercial rates for the hiring of PKS domestic vehicles. Such hire contracts are normally long term for two to three years.

(ii) With the revocation of the licensing system, industrial and factory vehicles are now occasionally used for international transit when industries require it. The scale of operations is unknown as no data is published, but it is felt to be small.

(iii) Prior to these changes the only Polish freight forwarder was C Hartwig SA. Liberalisation of the Polish economy has allowed a variety of freight forwarders to develop and in response Hartwig has diversified into international road haulage itself. It also provides the majority of work for PEKAES and Autotransport and thus competes with its own main customers. Hartwig is one hundred percent state owned, but is a prime candidate for early privatisation.

Currently Hartwig is organised into five main sections:

- Warsaw   (all air and East Europe)
- Gdansk   (sea)
- Gdynia   (sea and North Europe)
- Szczecin   (sea and West Europe)
- Katowice   (South Europe)

Each, theoretically at least, competes with each other for trade both in forwarding and haulage, although clear collaboration goes on in both vehicle usage and price setting. There is some

135

competition from a small number of private forwarding companies that have been established recently.

(iv)   There are also a large number of other operators now operating internationally, both state and privately owned. These include the fleet of Polish Ocean Line (POL) trucks, State owned and used to provide international transfer of containers from Gdansk and Szczecin; and a steel fabricators, formerly state owned and now purchased by an expatriate Pole from Australia for only US$200,000, now revitalised and remodelled, operating a fleet of ten vehicles in Europe carrying both its own and other products. There are also a growing number of one man/one vehicle private operators using, commonly, second hand Western made vehicles purchased from PEKAES.

Thus, some diversity has been brought to the international road haulage market place, but it remains limited in competitive structure despite continued moves to increase the level of privatisation and therefore competition.

PEKAES

PEKAES remains the dominant international haulier despite the moves made so far to diversity the provision of international services. Consequently we shall concentrate on PEKAES for much of the following discussion.

PEKAES is a company of some size in the world of road haulage. It owns some 1,200 tractors and rather more trailers of many types, the vast majority of which are West European made. It has operated since 1958 in virtually all West and East European markets, and compares favourably in size and organisation with Hungarocamion (Hungary) and Somat (Bulgaria). It is rather bigger then VEB Deutrans (DDR) and Romtrans (Romania); similar in size to Cesmad (Czechoslovakia). Somewhere between 60 and 70% of all contracts, by value, are with Polish customers as importers or more commonly, exporters. The remaining 30 to 40% of traffic originates from freight forwarding agents mainly in Western Europe.

Of the Polish originating commodities, 60% stems from the state-owned forwarder, Hartwig, noted earlier as now a competitor in international haulage. Consequently we may see a move away from this source in the near future. The majority of the other 40% of Polish originating traffic comes from newly constituted private freight forwarders which have increased dramatically from a very low level at the beginning of 1989 in response to the liberalisation of the Polish economy. A small proportion is attracted directly from industry (largely still state owned at mid 1990). Both categories are increasing and may thus compensate for any decline in Hartwig traffic that occurs.

PEKAES itself has diversified from the trucking market in response to the liberalised economy and the threats of competition from other operators in the international market place. Diversification includes the setting up of a freight forwarding section but aimed at hauliers only. Warehouse facilities have also been acquired and customs clearance, accounting and even travel agency work is now provided for customers. Not only is this aimed at providing a more diversified economic base, but also at reducing fees to intermediate agencies. Warehousing facilities in particular, are seen as a major way forward, and property has now been acquired in the west of Poland specifically for the West European market, to act as a transhipment depot from transfer of goods from local (East European) made trucks to Western made long distance vehicles. It will also play a part in establishing PEKAES as an international operator in major cross-trades between the West and the Soviet Union and between Scandinavia and Southern Europe and the Near and Middle East.

International destinations regularly served include all European countries, with some rather more frequently served than others.

In Western and Northern Europe the countries most served are those with the greatest economic links - particularly West Germany, the Netherlands and Belgium. Less frequently, but still regularly linked are Italy, Austria, France, Scandinavia and the UK; and occasionally and irregularly linked are the Iberian peninsula and Greece. The Republic of Ireland is not regularly covered.

The Near and Middle East is dominated by traffic to and from Iran, Iraq, Jordan, Syria, Turkey and Kuwait. This traffic is normally routed Poland-Czechoslovakia-Hungary- Romania-Bulgaria-Turkey and on; or less frequently Poland-Soviet Union-Turkey. One factor in the devolopment of this latter route is to overcome a permit shortage for transitting Czechoslovakia.

Overall, the Near and Middle East traffic is no longer a major proportion of traffic for two main reasons - the Iran/Iraq war, and the development of new competitors in the international road haulage market from Bulgaria and Turkey. On top of this, the economics of the market have collapsed, due to the horrendously low rates charged by the new competitors, so that they are now (1990) less than 50% of what they were ten years ago. In reality, the only Near and Middle East traffic that PEKAES actively encourages is when trucks would otherwise be idle and rates cover the marginal costs of transport alone. In some cases, even the marginal costs have not been met.

The East European road haulage market is far less important than might be realised at first. A number of problems exist which detract from this market:

(i)   Business with the Soviet Union - the dominant East European trading partner - is not easy, particularly in relation to the conversion of payments in roubles. The normal Soviet payments in 'transferable roubles', which in fact can only be used to purchase Soviet products, are next to useless as there are few (if any) Soviet products desired.

(ii)   Soviet trucks from the state owned Soyuz - transport international trucking company, charge extremely low prices due to state subsidy and thus are highly attractive compared with PEKAES for both Polish-USSR movements and cross trades. This is exacerbated by the convention in East Europe that rates charged are based on the country transited. Since the majority of Polish-USSR journeys are predominantly in the USSR, the low rates of the latter (noted above) predominate. The result is that 90% of all Poland-USSR trucking is undertaken by Soviet vehicles.

(iii)   Railway domination of international transport within Eastern Europe due to a combination of subsidised railways and historical precedent leaves little traffic to the road industry.

(iv)   Low levels of goods movements suited for road transport between East European countries, compared with that to Western Europe, makes road transit unattractive.

(v)   The attraction of hard currency earnings to the West encourages
        concentration of scarce truck resources in that market.

Clearly with the changes in East Europe taking place including currency
convertibility, developing economies, reduced subsidy, changing product
markets etc ... this will change in time. In the meantime, West European
markets remain dominant in contrast to the dominance of imports and
exports to the East.

The commodities carried are diverse, as might be expected, but largely
reflect the characteristics of the Polish economy. Thus, in the export
trade large quantities of wood products, glass, agricultural products,
textiles, fruit and vegetables and fruit products dominate, whilst in terms
of imports, the highest quantity of items are those of high technology and
consumer goods, and industrial machinery. Chemicals are moved in bulk
in both directions but PEKAES possesses no specialised chemical carriers
and Western hauliers or other Eastern hauliers are used in all cases. A
large number of temperature controlled vehicles are kept for carrying the
fruit and vegetable products.

In terms of trade with the European Community, Poland has benefitted
from a trade surplus since 1982. If Intra German trade is excluded (FDR
to DDR), Poland is the second trading partner of the Community in
Eastern Europe. Fluctuations in the volume of trade between Poland and
the European Community, however, have characterised the markets since
1982. In 1986, for example, imports from the Community to Poland
dropped by 77%, and exports to the Community by 13%. However, in
1988 and 1989 increases in both figures were recorded - for example, in
the first half of 1989 imports rose 20% and exports, 56%. Future
inflation controlling measures may damage this rise in trade as Polish
industry is exposed increasingly to market forces. This will have a clear
effect on trucking which has boomed with the increase in volumes since
1988.

As noted already, the vast majority of PEKAES trucks used in
international transport are of Western manufacture. All trips to and from
Western Europe are made by Western made trucks with Eastern
European vehicles (mainly Polish and USSR in origin) being reserved for
internal East European movements, and for some Polish sectors of
Western trips. Some 50% of the Western vehicles are Volvos (12), with
the remainder evenly split between Fiat/Iveco (Turbo Stars), Mercedes
(1625 and 1422) and Renault (TR305). Trailers (including tilt, box,

refrigerated, tanker, container frames, car transporter and low loader units) are variously manufactured including Fruehauf, Lohr, Kassbohrer, Magyar, Achleitner, Placenza, Trailor and Norfrig.

This diverse range of trailors and tractors is maintained for a number of reasons including , in particular, the commercial strength it gives PEKAES in purchasing negotiations; experience of varied performance characteristics of each type; and marketing advantages in the differing countries of Western Europe. Vehicles are garaged all over Poland to serve regional markets, but vehicle types are concentrated homogeneously within each depot to ensure consistency of service and maintenance and economies of scale in parts storage.

Western European trucks are used for a number of reasons, despite high initial costs and the need for hard currency:

- cheap to run in the long term;
- reliable;
- high quality of service;
- marketing;
- the majority of mileage is in Western Europe, therefore it is sensible to run 'local' trucks.

Polish trucking costs were constantly claimed to be similar to those of the West. Western vehicles are used and hence servicing, maintenance, repair and fuel consumption characteristics are comparable. Labour costs were claimed to be a relatively small proportion of total costs by comparison and hence, although labour is undoubtedly much cheaper, it is not a significant issue. However, clearly labour costs are cheaper and hence this may explain their comparative insignificance. Average wages for a PEKAES driver operating in the West are higher than those in the East of Europe averaging about 12,6000,000-16,200,000 zloty (>840-1080 : 1990) per year. There are no state controls on wages which are determined in negotiations between the drivers and PEKAES. New incentive schemes have been operating since 1989 based upon standard journey times and journey distances (for example, Warsaw-Paris return is six days). A daily allowance is paid to the driver for each standard day away whereby if the journey time is exceeded, no extra is paid unless an acceptable reason is given (for example a breakdown). If the journey is completed in less than the standard time, the driver still receives the standard allowance. In 1990 an additional incentive scheme based on distance was introduced, based on a standard daily drive of 450 km. If this standard is exceeded, pay is increased; if not reached, pay is reduced. Tachographs are used on all Western vehicles and clearly, Western European laws on driver's hours and mileage have to be recognised. New equipment is being introduced in 1990, which will enable PEKAES to analyse driver and vehicle performance.

All PEKAES trucks are covered by state arranged third party insurance and the Green Card scheme. However, insurance costs differ from those of the West. Domestic charges in January 1990 were 3,000 zloty for each tractor and each trailer per year (about 20p). International charges were substantially higher - tractors 165,000 zloty per year, and trailers 135,000 zloty (about >11 and >9 each per year). Clearly this discrepancy compared with Western insurance premiums, is a notable one.

Fuel costs are less of a major issue since much of the kilometrage covered by PEKAES trucks is bound to be in Western Europe, and thus fuel costs will be comparable. All trucks carry fuel capacities of 400 or 600 litres. It is pointless for the trucks to have fuel capacities bigger than this since many transit countries (and in particular West Germany) have laws that constrain the import of diesel fuel. January 1990 Polish diesel costs were 1,900 zloty per litre (about 12} pence). Inflation, however, continues to play havoc with the price of fuel - for example, it doubled in price on 31 December 1989.

Vehicle taxation costs are very low in Poland and form an insignificant burden.

Overall it was claimed that PEKAES profits were not abnormally high in Western trading - although it is very difficult to substantiate this. The availability of backhauls is a major determinant of profit, and one that causes considerable problems for the Poles due to the nature of their economic problems. Exports are considerably greater in size and weight than imports, and the future economic prospects will exacerbate the disparity. If backhauls are available, profits are good. If not, they are low or non-existent. PEKAES openly admits that 70% of their trucks return to Poland empty, and of the remaining 30% a proportion acquire backhauls for only part of the return journey.

The cost structure outlined above indicates that PEKAES is a competitive organisation in the Western haulage market. Earnings in 1989 were about 2DM per kilometre operated. Fuel costs in Western Europe were about 0.4DM per km, with the remaining 1.6DM per km having to cover all other overheads, plus any profit.

Commentators from the Academy of Economics, Katowice, claimed that Polish international haulage was very profitable, producing a rate of return of 30% on investment, frequently in hard currency. However, this has been due largely to the expansion of trade since liberalisation in 1988, and thus may be hit badly by the economic recession that looms in 1990 and beyond.

However, much of the profit from these successful Western operations in the past has not been reinvested in the industry as it should have been, to maximise returns to the Polish economy and trucking industry. This was largely as a consequence of the state's needs for hard currency to finance the import of products unavailable in the East. PEKAES (amongst all other industries) until recently could keep little of the hard currency earned, although what it did retain it did reinvest in new Western vehicles in particular and to purchase fuel in the West, and to provide subsistence to drivers.

All the above in relation to hard currency earnings, has changed since 1 January 1990 as the Polish zloty is now convertible. This has made trade administratively much easier, but vastly more expensive. The zloty was worth 150.14z to the US$ in December, 1985. By January 1990 it was 9,000 to the US$. Hence, hard currency is now freely available even through zloty earnings, albeit at an appalling (yet realistic) rate of exchange.

Previously all modes of international transport carrying goods for Western exporters to Poland, or importers from Poland, would have earned hard currency, which was repatriated. However, PEKAES was allowed to retain only 50% of that currency in hard format; the rest had to return to the state in exchange for zloty's at the official (punitive) rate of exchange. Not only that, but there existed a limited list of officially approved goods that hard currency could be spent on, highly restricted in range and nature. The result, amongst other things, was a lack of incentive to earn more hard currency. It was a system applied to all Polish industry regardless of economic activity, but one that was inconsistent in the way that it was applied in terms of retention of hard currency earnings. For example, whilst PEKAES might have had a 50% retention level, another industry might have had 85% or 35%. The proportions allocated were seemingly arbitrarily decided.

The new arrangements, from 1 January 1990 are that only one bank account is allowed in zlotys. All hard currencies are paid into the State Bank and it is returned, largely in full, at the appropriate official exchange rate to the company concerned, which is now free to spend that income as it wishes, including reconverting it back to a hard currency of choice, again at the prevailing official rate.

Two contrasting views have emerged of the new arrangements:

(i)   Company planners (including PEKAES) can now plan more easily, using hard currency, and have incentives to earn more. Inconsistencies between industries have been removed, and all companies are placed on the same footing.

(ii)   But, due to tradition and lack of experience, some managers in many industries prefer the old system to which they are accustomed. In particular, the zloty rate is now variable and consequently unpredictable.

        Also, the new system is designed to increase exports at the expense of imports by making the zloty/hard currency conversion rates punitive. This does nothing to help increase the availability of hard currency and will indirectly hinder the acquisition of backhauls.

One issue that has proved very hard to establish is the level of state subsidy to the trucking industry as a whole, and to the international trucking sector (ie PEKAES in particular). PEKAES freely admit that in the past there have been indirect subsidies in the form of cheap loans, free accommodation, subsidised labour and so on. However, it is now claimed that the only subsidy left, until recently, was in the form of tax rebates on profits which were available to a limited number of industrial and commercial sectors, including PEKAES. Consequently, PEKAES must make a commercial profit or go bankrupt. Since January 1990, even this rebate has been removed. Doubts remain, however, with the infrastructure of the company largely state owned and the employees largely state employed, just how much indirect subsidy really remains. However, subsidies have been reduced and the state safety net which previously existed, is much less reliable. The short-term effect may be to require PEKAES to pay higher wages (to cover inflationary costs caused by subsidy renewal), and higher costs for accommodation and other facilities. This will have an obvious effect on their ability to undercut Western hauliers in the future. Ultimately in the longer term, unemployment should reduce wage claims thus making them rather more competitive. The situation for the future remains unsure.

In terms of international haulage cross-trading, Poland traditionally has been a transit country between the USSR and DDR/West Europe, and between Scandinavia and the Mediterranean/South Europe. However, in the last decade a number of events have tended to reduce the significance of this activity. In particular, the period of martial law in Poland in the 1980's encouraged previous cross-trade and transit movements previously using Polish territory, to travel either through the DDR (for north-south, Mediterranean-Scandinavian links) or via the USSR-DDR vehicle ferry between Riga and Rostock, across the Baltic Sea. The result has been a dramatic fall in cross-trade and transit traffic for PEKAES. However, the operator and State Ministry view it as a sizeable potential market that should be recovered and consequently there are plans to develop a new network of motorways in Poland to encourage the traffic back (and also to help develop the Polish economy). The main routes partially under construction or planned include:

> Berlin-Warsaw-Brest (USSR)
> Krakow-Katowice-DDR
> Gdansk-Warsaw
> Szczecin-South of Poland-Czechoslovakia

Clearly cost is a major factor in all these plans (at an estimated 50m zloty per km; January 1990).

Unaccompanied loads, whereby the trailer is carried by a tractor to a port or railway terminal and then detached to continue movement by ship or rail freight vehicle to its ultimate destination or to meet another tractor from another operator, are not viewed as an attractive option by PEKAES. This contrasts, for example, with the Soviet Union transporters who normally use this method for trailers destined for the UK, Eire or ports of Scandinavia.

PEKAES viewed it relatively cheaply to pay a driver to accompany the load (especially compared with Western road haulage labour rates), plus the extra ferry or fuel cost. It was also a more secure option and consequently more attractive to the customer. Goods were pinpointed most of the time and accompanied at all times. A number of other points also made it more attractive - demurrage on trailers was never incurred, loading and unloading costs were avoided and overall revenue to PEKAES was increased as the quality of service provided was higher. Finally, insurance costs were lower and disputes over breakages and losses easier to sort out when the driver was on hand. To quote PEKAES, 'trucking is supposed to be door to door and therefore it is better if it is accompanied'. Consequently, PEKAES only use unaccompanied loads to Sweden where permits were strictly limited, and some loads could only be sent if the trailer was unaccompanied.

Piggyback transport (lorry on rail) was a different option. Poland has already invested relatively heavily in this market with specialised rail facilities existing between Gdansk, Austria and Czechoslovakia. This accommodates a major movement of trailers from Scandinavia and the Baltic to Southern and Central Europe. Two trainloads are carried each week of the year.

However, the Polish economy is slowly changing and whereas once as much traffic as possible was directed towards the railways, under new legislation this is no longer the case and industrial consumers and producers will now choose as they wish in terms of transport mode. Commodity characteristics are also slowly changing with more high-tech, manufactured and perishable products clearly more suited to road transport. This in turn will help PEKAES to expand its markets at the expense of previously rail-directed freight.

PEKAES was also well aware of the impending Single European Market after 1992, and believe that enormous opportunities will emerge as a result. Consequently, they have formed two joint-stock companies in the Netherlands and the UK which operate international haulage vehicles, profits from which are allocated proportionately to PEKAES and the other owners and are repatriated to Poland in hard currency. The two companies are:

Vecto (Netherlands) - with sixteen trucks, 90% PEKAES owned, 10% Netherlands

ETS (European Truck Services) (UK).
Part of Amandus Shipping with five trucks, 50% PEKAES owned, 50% UK.

Both concentrate on the UK/Netherlands-European Community markets, but can and are used for USSR/Poland journeys when demand requires it, and collaborate directly with PEKAES including vehicle exchanges, providing cleaning and mechanical facilities, and marketing and agency services. Another option is the co-operation of services - for example, linking Poland-Netherlands (PEKAES) with Netherlands-Spain (Vecto) tractors.

Conclusions

PEKAES represents the major operator in Polish international trucking by far, even though competition from other state hauliers and private concerns now exists. The private sector, in particular, is economically fragile and with the severe constraints and problems of the Polish economy is one that will be characterised by a succession of bankruptcies in the near future. PEKAES by contrast, although having the potential to fail, is supported by a substantial state system, albeit with reduced subsidies, and almost guaranteed markets, and a large and experienced marketing and administrative network. It is thus unlikely to fail.

It is a relatively modern trucking company (compared with most of the rest of Eastern Europe, and with CMEA industry in general), with an understanding of the changes occurring throughout Europe and the Single European Market in particular. It will continue to benefit from low labour costs for the foreseeable future.

Drawbacks include the deficiencies of East European bureaucracy which largely remain, and the deficiencies of a Polish industrial market that it serves. Continuing hidden and inestimable subsidies may help to cushion the affects of these problems. Overall, PEKAES has the potential to become a competitive and large-scale international trucking company in direct competition with Western hauliers, and if the Polish economy revives it may well prosper. What is urgently needed is marketing, financial and organisational/management advice and training to revise their company procedures and structures in a highly competitive market environment. It is in this way that Western aid can help PEKAES prosper, survive the short term crises of Poland and thus contribute to the revival of Eastern Europe as a whole.

9 Conclusions

Introduction

This text has described the results of an analysis of the operation, planning and policies of international road haulage in Eastern Europe during a period of enormous economic and political change in the region. The result of these changes is that the objectives of the work have been extended as it has progressed, incorporating not only how the East European haulage industry competes with the West and the conditions under which it operates, but also how it can be helped in surviving competition from the West, and how it can aid its own local industrial redevelopment as market forces bite.

In this concluding section, the aim is threefold. Firstly, to examine briefly the way the Single European Market, in place from the 1 January 1993, will affect the operation of East European and Community hauliers; and how knowledge of its arrival has affected haulier planning already. Secondly, the degree of unfair trading that has been promoted in the Eastern Bloc and to what extent it continues even in the new economic climate; and thirdly, the ways that the European Community and its Member States can help the international haulage industry in the east to survive and prosper in the commercial environment that is about to develop.

The Single European Market

It is not the intention here to describe and analyse in detail the moves towards the completion of the internal market, proposed under the Single European Act. Instead, a few brief comments on its basic aims will be made followed by an analysis of its effects upon the East European road haulage industry.

The 31st December, 1992, is the date set by the European Community for the completion of the single internal market as defined by the single European Act of July 1987:-

"An area without frontiers in which the free movement of goods, persons, services and capital is assured, in accordance with the provisions of the Treaty of Rome."

The impetus for the creation of the internal market was not only the Treaty of Rome, but also realisation of the massive shifts in geopolitical landscape, intensified competition and accelerating technological change worldwide. Pressure to find a common response grew, plus a realisation that most Member States could not achieve economic growth and compete worldwide on their own.

The Single European Act requires an internal market to be created by the end of 1992, and this in itself has meant that an enormous amount of legislation has had to be agreed and passed by the Council of Ministers, to ensure that activities within the European Community are conducted in a harmonised fashion. These measures will affect all economic activities including road haulage - and ultimately will create a single consumer market of 320 million people free from internal barriers and the problems of dealing with 12 sets of national legislation, rather than one, harmonised throughout the Community. This will aid road hauliers in a number of ways:-

(i)   the overall market for freight will be bigger due to the increased prosperity that the single market will generate and the increase in trade and traffic that cross-border industrial collaboration will generate;

(ii)   the transport market will become more dynamic and competitive. Experience of deregulation in the USA has shown that successful companies must be alive to changes and capable of quick reaction. It is likely that there will be increased competition in the industry, creating additional economies of scale and concentrations of expertise;

(iii)   real prices will drop, some suggest by up to 15-20%, almost immediately.

All this means a more efficient, cheaper and more flexible/adaptable road haulage industry - which will engage in both intra- and extra-European Community trade, the latter in part at least, to and from Eastern Europe. Clearly, a more efficient road haulage industry in Western Europe will place great pressure on those operators from Eastern Europe to become more efficient to retain or expand their market share. As we have seen earlier, some East European operators (particularly Bulgaria, Hungary and Poland) have reacted positively to the creation of the Single European Market in developing affiliate companies, and extensive networks of agents and representatives in the European Community, in that they benefit from the trade growth of post 1992.

Overall, the effect of the creation of the internal market will be to make the EC haulage industry more efficient, more aware of the concept of quality of service, more flexible to industrial needs, cheaper and more able to respond to East European needs as it becomes more market orientated. It will provide more competition for haulage operators in the East who are losing in the main, much of the protection from competitors that they have enjoyed whilst virtual arms of the State Ministry. Whilst East European industry declines, the traditional markets of the Eastern Bloc hauler will decline as well.

As the same industrial sectors recover in time, the value of quality of service (timing, speed, reliability, etc) will become paramount, and the Western haulier, experienced in these market demands, will inevitably gain traffic at the expense of the East. Meanwhile, hard currency will continue to be in demand by hauliers in the East, to spend on acquiring new vehicles from the West - and yet will be less available as the Eastern Bloc declines. All this points to a very difficult period for Eastern Bloc hauliers as they come to terms with state withdrawals, and economic decline, and consequently a need for help from the West for them to survive and prosper as part of the necessary industrial and commercial success needed in East Europe.

Some Conclusions

This research has covered a very wide range of issues but the conclusions drawn out here will concentrate upon the international road haulage market alone. A number of conclusions can be drawn from the case studies presented earlier of Bulgaria, Czechoslovakia, Hungary and Poland, and from the incidental information gained from the DDR and Romania:-

(i)   The research has had to modify and add to its original primary objectives of gaining an understanding of the business methods and organisation of East European international hauliers in the light of potential unfair trading practices, to one which also accommodates the needs of the haulage industry in the Eastern Bloc as it attempts to come to terms with the new market economy. Both strands are still relevant - the Eastern Bloc hauliers still continue to practice the way they always have in East-West trade, but now additionally, must conform at home to the demands of the new political and economic climate.

(ii)   Stemming from (i), it is clear from direct consultation with senior managers in Hungary, Poland, Bulgaria, Czechoslovakia, Romania and the DDR that progress will be very slow, particularly in changing attitudes to business and the methods that have been adopted in trading with the West over the last 20-30 years. Hence, traffic will continue to be encouraged into East European vehicles by a combination of subsidy, state traffic direction and trading conditions (particularly the cif/fob practice), whilst the East European operators adapt to the idea of commercialism. The vast majority of managers, technicians, drivers and so on, are the same as were employed by the companies prior to the political and economic changes - educated and experienced in techniques and attitudes under the old regime's rules. Their approach to western markets will change very slowly. Hence it is fairly safe to say that the unfair trading practices that were identified in the ECSEC Report of 1977 will continue for some time yet and will continue to place pressure on western hauliers attempting to gain a fair share of European Community-CMEA trade.

(iii)   The hard currency issue remains largely unaltered. With the exception of Poland, where the zloty became convertible on the 1 January 1990, all the Eastern Bloc countries have unconvertible currencies and will continue to be anxious to obtain hard currency at almost any cost. International road haulage is a relatively easy way of earning hard currency and hence, it will continue to be used in this way, pricing low to obtain the precious commodity.

Even in Poland direct hard currency earnings remain very attractive as the zloty has been heavily devalued. Whilst the problems of hard currency remain in the East, there is little prospect of the international haulage industry changing its trading practices and it will continue to operate at below true cost to earn hard currency for itself and the state. This will be particularly the case for those hauliers still totally owned and managed by State Ministries (eg, Romania), but is also true of those currently on the way towards commercial independence - such as Hungarocamion, Pekaes and Somat, who need hard currency to purchase new western vehicles to attract more western traffic and hence, more hard currency earnings.

(iv)   However, apart from Romania, where any reliable information is very thin on the ground, there is little evidence that direct subsidy of international road haulage takes place. Every senior manager spoken to denied the existence of direct subsidy payments by the state either now or, in most cases, in the past. The subsidy issue is more subtle than this, rather more difficult to pinpoint and possibly one poorly understood by the senior managers of the industry themselves.

(v)   Indirect subsidies undoubtedly do exist and are the main mechanism for aiding the international haulage industry at the moment, and has been for many years. No direct evidence is available. However, we can point towards a number of cases where indirect subsidy is undoubtedly occurring.

Firstly, many of the international haulage operators in the Eastern Bloc share facilities (including vehicles in some cases - for example Cesmad/Csad in Czechoslovakia; Volan in Hungary) for maintenance, servicing, cleaning etc, with national road haulage operators, and in some cases with national road passenger operations. The latter services are openly and heavily subsidised in all East European countries and there appears to be no attempt to make international hauliers pay a true commercial price for the facilities they use - hence an indirect subsidy.

Secondly, there is little evidence to support the view that facilities such as buildings, land, catering, cleaning, telephones and other administrative and technical services are provided at true cost. International hauliers utilise these facilities provided at below cost (at times at no cost) by the state.

Thirdly, the rates charged by the state for insurance, road tax, fuel tax, vehicle tax and for East European manufactured trucks, are very low and certainly below the cost of provision, vehicle manufacturing cost and so on. Taking East European trucks, including makes such as Liaz and Raba, used on some western trips, these manufacturers are heavily subsidised by the state lowering vehicle cost, and thus providing an indirect subsidy to the operators who use them.

(vi) Western hauliers do not benefit from these indirect subsidies to anything like the same extent. It is true that some European countries have tax regimes below the true costs that trucks impose on the community, but nothing like to the same extent that it occurs in the East. Some vehicle manufacturers in the West are state owned and probably state aided (eg, Renault, France), and hence a limited amount of indirect subsidy enters the market. Western operators are unable to take advantage of the low cost East European trucks as any that they might wish to purchase would be sold at higher cost, and in hard currency. The same type of discrimination follows in the sale of fuel, maintenance facilities, servicing, repairs, cleaning and so on - available only at higher cost and in hard currency. Hence Western operators have fewer indirectly subsidised facilities available to them in the West, than Eastern hauliers in the East, and cannot avail themselves of the East European subsidised services. Meanwhile, Eastern hauliers can avail themselves of partially subsidised Western manufactured vehicles - as long as they have the hard currency to do it.

(vii)   Trading conditions remain a very important constraint on Western involvement in East-West traffic. FTOs continue to operate as an arm of the state in all Eastern Bloc countries even where competition has been allowed through private freight forwarders and direct industrial trading - for example, Hungary and Poland.   These FTOs continue to dictate transport nationality by insisting wherever possible, on contracts being cif (exports from the East) and fob (imports to the East). Industry in the West is attracted to the Eastern haulier by the low rates charged. Western importers and exporters are not compelled to contract trade on the same terms as the East - and hence the Eastern Bloc dominates the market.   Independent freight forwarders do now exist, plus the direct organisation of transport by industry - but old attitudes remain and there is understandably some subtle state pressure to continue the cif/fob practices.   Meanwhile the majority of industry in the East remains state owned - and must do so for some years to come. Hence there is an obvious pressure from state industry, to encourage state and private forwarders to help international hauliers from the East. This issue of trading conditions remains central to the imbalance of trade - although it is not the only factor involved as we shall see.

(viii)   These trading arrangements make backhauls very difficult to acquire for Western hauliers in the East - and hence make transport provision very expensive.

Hauliers from the West were previously unable to acquire backhauls except through state run FTOs, and consequently received very few. With increased freedom and competition the situation may be a little better and Western hauliers and freight forwarders can now establish representatives and agents in the East to look for loads, which previously was illegal. However, the situation remains far from easy.

Meanwhile, Eastern hauliers and freight forwarders have always been able to be represented in the West and operators such as Hungarocamion, Pekaes, Cesmad and Somat have for many years had their own employees in the West in strategic locations (for example Rotterdam and Hamburg), looking out for traffic and backhauls, helping to make their operations more profitable.   Hence their relatively high level of backhauls -

commonly 60-80%.

(ix)   State interference with international haulage is not confined to that of indirect subsidy. Most of the international hauliers and industry continues to have senior managers appointed by the state - clearly under pressure to continue state policies with respect to trading practices, vehicle acquisition, charging policy, hard currency deals and so on.

(x)   Many of the East European international hauliers understand the needs of the Western haulage market, at least to a certain extent, and have recognised that to retain their share of the haulage market they need to operate reasonably good quality vehicles, well maintained and to provide a high level of quality of service in terms of timing, reliability, vehicle design and so on.   Hence, the widespread use of Western vehicles by Hungarocamion, Pekaes and Somat, the level of technical facilities provided for these vehicles and Western operators who wish to use them, and the level of marketing and representative provision in Western strategic centres. Price is certainly not the only issue in hard currency acquisition, and indirect subsidy is used by East European states to enable the Eastern Bloc hauliers to acquire the facilities they need to maintain a high market share.   Hungarian, Polish and Bulgarian vehicles are of particularly good quality, well maintained and relatively new. Cesmad of Czechoslovakia seems less aware of the needs of Western industry, and still operates many East European manufactured vehicles in Western Europe and exchanges national and international vehicles at will. Romania, due to its chequered recent history, still operates only Romanian made 'Roman' vehicles and is an important element of East-West trade.   However, due to its trading practices, it continues to monopolise the small Romania-EC road trade.

(xi)   Wages paid to East European international truck drivers are good in comparison with those paid generally in Eastern Europe, and made exceptional by their partial payment in hard currency, to cover costs in the West and as a privilege. Hence competition for jobs is intense. However, compared with West European rates, they are very low.   Recent figures from Bulgaria suggest an average monthly salary of >100 - compared with the UK, with an average 10-12 times that

154

amount. This lies behind the other main reason why East European hauliers obtain a larger share of international trade between East and West and why they find it much easier to fill their quota of bilateral permits. Clearly, if wages are that much lower, rates for transport can be considerably below those of the West and still cover costs. Undoubtedly, as the market economy bites, East European wages costs and prices will rise, but it will be many years (if ever) before both East and West European wages equate.

(xii)   A number of issues are raised by truck fuel in Eastern Europe. Cost of fuel are considerably lower in the East, then in the West, and although it is of lower quality, this undoubtedly helps the East European international haulier. This is especially the case because West European hauliers cannot take advantage of the low fuel costs in the East as they are compelled to buy vouchers in hard currency to obtain fuel, and then at a higher cost than locally. However, despite this, fuel is not a major issue in the disparity in trade carryings between East and West. Restrictions on fuel imports, particularly in West Germany - a major transit and destination/origin country in Western Europe, constrain the benefits which Eastern hauliers can obtain from low fuel costs and much fuel still has to be purchased in the West at West European prices.

(xiii) Taxation is another issue of small concern in the disparity of costs between East and West hauliers. Road and vehicle taxation is minimal in the Eastern Bloc and in some cases does not exist at all. In the West it is major cost element particularly in the United Kingdom. Moves are already beginning in the East to introduce a system of higher taxation charges for hauliers, but it is unlikely to be a quick process and is very unlikely to bring the costs of taxation to match those of infrastructure provision in the near future - unlike in the European Community. However, compared with the disparity in wage costs, this is not a major issue.

(xiv)   Insurance costs are similarly very low in the East and in some cases are free (eg, Romania). A small element in cost disparity between East and West once again, but coupled with the disparity in fuel and taxation costs, helps to make East European operations that much cheaper. Once again, the market economy will eventually force up insurance costs to a more commercial rate - in time.

(xv)   Alternative markets to the West, for East European operators, are not strong. The Near and Middle East markets have died away dramatically due to the effects of the Iran/Iraq war and the impact of a huge growth in Turkish hauliers operating at low rates, even lower than those of most of East Europe. The only East European haulier to remain, significantly in this market is Somat (Bulgaria) who are involving particularly in cross-trading and transferring loads in Sofia from both East and West European trucks, and transiting them onwards via Turkey and the Black Sea. The Gulf Crisis of 1990 has done nothing to help this market recover, which once, for Hungarian and Czechoslovakian operators, was their major source of income.

The East European internal market is a small one due to the poor infrastructure of the region, the absence of hard currency earnings and the tradition of rail orientated traffic. None of the East European international operators are particularly interested in the internal CMEA market, using it as a means of filling trucks which would otherwise be idle. The main trading partner of all the six countries is the USSR, who continue to dominate the small amount of road traffic that exists - largely by operating at very low rates and due to the convoluted administrative structure for haulage that exists within the CMEA. The decline in Eastern industrial markets in the short-term will do nothing to encourage EastEuropean international road haulage and hence this market is bound to remain insignificant compared with that of the West.

(xvi)   Privatisation is a very current issue for the international hauliers in Eastern Europe, particularly in Czechoslovakia, Poland and Hungary. All six of the international hauliers under review are currently (1/1/1990) state owned, but moves in Czechoslovakia in particular should result in a privatised operation by the end of 1990. Details of privatisation are unknown as yet and could involve sale to the state itself. In Poland and Hungary, both state hauliers are profitable (albeit thanks partly to state aid) and thus prime elements for sale to the private sector. However, despite moves in many sectors, particularly in Hungary, the prospects for early sales do not look good. The reason for this is that the state needs hard currency urgently and international road haulage is a relatively easy way of acquiring it - hence the state is loathe to sell off one of its more profitable and economic ventures. Eventually, it seems likely that in the more progressive East European countries, sales will take place resulting in a more efficient and dynamic set of operators to compete with the West. Rates, however, will undoubtedly rise to compensate any loss of indirect subsidy or preferential treatment by the state. One notable effect may be the abandonment of East European markets where profits (if any) are low, and a concentration on Western Europe. There are no realistic prospects of privatisation in Bulgaria at the moment, where the state continues to hold onto its ownership of Somat, and in Romania there are few prospects even in the long-term, partly because there would be few buyers of an industry in such poor condition, in a country of economic chaos.

(xvii)   Competition has increased dramatically in Eastern Europe in international markets for road haulage, but from an almost non-existent base. In Hungary, in particular, there is active competition, albeit on a small scale and in limited markets (especially West Germany and Eastern Europe) from the national state haulier Volan, whilst in Poland, attempts to establish a competitive market are also centred around the national haulier Autotransport and the state freight forwarder Hertwig. Private operators are also growing very quickly in number in both countries.

Some doubts must be experienced about the true level of competition that is being developed. In both Hungary and Poland the main competitors are also state owned and have close relationships with the established international hauliers. The development of private operators is partly a response to the availability of numerous old second-hand vehicles, and the rise in unemployment. Doubts have to be expressed about the ability of the market to provide traffic for all the new entrants. Their ability to survive may be made even more difficult by the nature of the established largest operators (eg, Hungarocamion and Pekaes) who dominate the market and have numerous state connections and an extensive representative network abroad.

Competition can do nothing but good for the international

haulage industry in the East in general, but needs to be developed to a much greater extent than has occurred so far and needs to ensure equal chances of traffic for all competitors. Inevitably, some of the smaller, independent operators will not survive the traumas of the market to come.

(xviii)   Cross-trading is a major activity of parts of the East European road haulage industry, particularly the Bulgarians who through Somat, have developed an expertise in serving the Middle and Near East markets for customers whose traffic origin is commonly West Europe. This traffic is either picked up (for example) in West Germany and then transported via Bulgaria - which gives Somat extra traffic rights to cross-trade and which is convenient in this market as it lies naturally on the route - or is transhipped in Sofia from West or East European trucks and taken on from there. Other East European countries cross-trade when it is convenient and easy; for example, there is a reasonable amount picked up by Hungarocamion trucks returning from Turkey or Greece, travelling via Romania and taken to the Baltic ports; whilst Pekaes are involved in traffic between Western Europe (particularly West Germany) and the Soviet Union. However, for most of the East European truckers it is not a major part of their business, which remains between the home country and West Europe generally (and vice versa).

(xix)   The main West European markets are undoubtedly found in West Germany for all the East European haulage companies followed a long way after by the North European ports located in Belgium and the Netherlands for transhipment either as containers or trailers to the UK, Scandinavia or the USA/Canada and further afield. Significant markets, particularly for Hungary, Czechoslovakia and Poland, lie in the Italian ports of Trieste and Genoa and to a certain extent the French port of Marseille/Fos, again for onward transportation, and to Austria. Much further down the destination list are direct shipments to France, Scandinavia, UK, Italy, Greece and Turkey. Finally, occasional loads (sometimes on a regular basis) are sent to Spain, Portugal, Luxembourg, Switzerland and Denmark. Eire is the smallest of the market served directly for obvious reasons of distance and market size. A lot of the internal international East European work is to the ports of

Gdansk and Szcezin in Poland (from Hungary and Czechoslovakia), and to the Black Sea ports of Constanta (Romania), Varna and Burgas (Bulgaria) (from Hungary, Czechoslovakia and Poland), but much of this latter work is monopolised by Romanian and Bulgarian hauliers as backhauls from the rest of Eastern Europe.

This pattern of trade is likely to continue, and only the area previously occupied by the DDR will increase traffic dramatically and, in the short term, after reunification with the West from 3 October 1990.

(xx)   Competition from rail and inland waterway continues to be very strong in Eastern Europe due to tradition and the belief in the inherent economies of scale of the rail mode. The operation of market forces and moves towards goods traffic which are more roads orientated (for example, high tech, high value commodities) will begin to erode this dominance in time, as will the increase in the importance of the concept of quality of service which has been misunderstood and underestimated in the past. Road transport, although inherently more expensive per kilometre, can be more flexible, accurate and reliable and if well organised (compared with railways), quicker. It will, thus, attract an increasingly large share of the market bringing benefits to both West and East European hauliers.

(xxi)   However, this increase in the use of road services may be outweighed by the collapse of the East European economies - and particularly their industries - creating a decline in commodities to be both imported and exported. In the short and medium term, all five remaining East European nations - Bulgaria, Czechoslovakia, Hungary, Poland and Romania - face problems of declining industrial output, rising inflation, devalued currencies, unemployment and heavy international indebtedness. Only Poland has anything that is like a convertible currency. Each, therefore, faces a crisis in industry, commerce and social conditions, presenting problems for international road haulage.

The prospects are very poor - the market is declining, costs are rising dramatically, and overall, one can see no real prospect in the short term, of much of the industry surviving without change. Aid from the West may help to cushion various blows, but part of the effect of the conditions attached to this aid (a move towards market economies) will be to expose international road haulage more to true commercial life. Purely by chance, this may present Western hauliers with more choice of obtaining a greater share of East-West traffic as Eastern Bloc hauliers find they have to raise prices and cannot find the hard currency needed to invest in the new vehicles and facilities required.

(xxii)   Another problem that has been noted earlier is the need for improved infrastructure in the East, particularly highways. Eastern European road hauliers cannot hope to meet the needs of a market economy with a highway infrastructure that is inadequate and far below Western standards. Western aid will once more help here, but a lot needs to be done and soon if the industry is to be able to contribute to economic recovery. Estimates for the DDR alone are some DM 2 billion to raise the standards of highways to anything like that of the West.

(xxiii)   In terms of the impact of 1992 and the implementation of the Single European Market, East Europe has begun to react already and has recognised the growth in West European international road haulage that will occur as a result of a stronger European Community industry as a whole. In particular, the effects can be noted in Hungary and Poland. Hungarocamion, for example, have established three affiliate companies in the EC (in Italy, the UK and Luxembourg) to operate international haulage vehicles, to obtain backhauls for Hungarocamion trucks, and to provide servicing, maintenance and administrative facilities for Hungarian (and other) trucks. Pekaes have similar developments in hand. This is a clear example of how these two reasonably well organised and structured companies will survive East European redevelopment and adapt to the new internal and Common Market. However, the moves taking place elsewhere are very few - particularly in Czechoslovakia and Romania - and there seems to be little recognition of the effects the Single European Act will have upon European trucking - or the lack of opportunities to do much about it.

Apart from the acquisition of companies within the EC area, little else has been achieved by East European hauliers to react currency remains in short supply, the East European economies are in decline, and the hauliers must sit and wait for developments to take place, as they happen.

(xxiv) Few of the international haulage companies operating from East Europe have moved beyond the confines of road haulage, and into new markets of warehousing, logistics and other related activities. Even Hungarocamion, (and Pekaes) the most dynamic of the six, have developed only limited warehousing facilities and have not even considered the provision of related logistic services such as fleet planning, route planning and scheduling, packaging, dedicated fleets and more, now so common in the West.

This is a field of activity in which the Eastern Bloc is in some need of help from the West. The East is renowned for its appalling distribution and logistical network with enormous losses of perishable goods, and delays in delivery, accompanied by a low quality of service overall.

It is an area that Western logistics companies are already actively examining in terms of setting up distribution and related services as the market opens up. In time, undoubtedly, the more advanced international hauliers in the East will move towards logistics as Eastern industry begins to demand higher qualities of service, attuned to their needs, and recognises the links between production, marketing and distribution. The less progressive - for example Romtrans (Romania) - will take considerably longer to realise the needs and to adapt to market needs, and there seems little prospect of developments in this area even in the medium term.

(xxv) Both Hungarocamion and Pekaes have, however, recognised the value of selling the commercial and technical facilities they possess for their own operations, including vehicle cleaning, maintenance, repair and servicing, legal and professional services, financial services and more. These services are now available, at true commercial cost, to international and national operators of all kinds. Thus Hungarocamion operates maintenance and servicing facilities as agents for Mercedes-Benz and Iveco Ford, providing all related services to any trucks of that make who wish to make use of them.

to any trucks of that make who wish to make use of them. Western hauliers are charged in hard currency, Eastern hauliers in local currency (in this case, Forints). Hungarocamion also have shares in a 'truck stop' facility near Budapest, adjacent to a major motorway junction, providing driver facilities such as beds, food and washing. It is predominantly used by cross-trading Turks but is available to anyone. Pekaes offer similar services to trucks and drivers in Poland, but these examples are still few and far between.

(xxvi) The East European haulage industry is in need of considerable help from the West. This help is not only financial, but also primarily economic, organisational, managerial and technical, to enable it to survive in a harsh commercial environment with no indirect subsidy, no direction of traffic, fierce competition and declining markets.

Not all of East European international trucking will survive the new environment, and undoubtedly as commercialism bites, the stronger companies will attempt to capture the markets of the weak. Many private and cooperative hauliers also will be unable to find sufficient traffic to maintain a profitable profile, particularly in Poland and Hungary where they have grown in number very quickly.

However, these problems may be lessened or at least pass more quickly, if the West can help in the most appropriate way.

First and foremost, more information and understanding of East European trucking is needed. There remains a very notable lack of data about the operating companies which, although improved upon in this report, presents continuing problems. Many of the companies involved are very willing to cooperate - particularly a range of operators from large to small, in Poland, Hungary and Bulgaria. Rather less cooperation is evident from Czechoslovakia and Romania. It is very important, if a significant part of East European industry is to survive and serve its national production industries, that there is a regular exchange of information, which is kept up to date, and that more is uncovered about business practices in the haulage sector.

Secondly, education and training in modern logistical and distribution techniques and practices is also essential. Even the more dynamic East European operators, lack the skills, information and experience to develop their companies to compete in the commercial market. They have rudimentary business and marketing skills but nothing to compare with Western hauliers. If Eastern industry is to redevelop, it needs a modern and efficiently run distribution sector. In Romania and Czechoslovakia in particular, the skills are notably absent. Educational facilities and experience are not available in the East to provide this training and Western help is urgently needed.

Thirdly, there is a chronic need for managerial and organisational advice to restructure the international haulage industry, to obtain the most from new logistical and distribution skills that will have been adopted. Current structures stem directly from the economic practices dominant pre-1989, characterised by a lack of local decision-making and a failure to innovate.

Finally, there are technical needs. Although some operators (particularly Hungarian, Polish and Bulgarian) possess a large number of Western-made vehicles, many need replacing fairly urgently. In the case of Cesmad and Romtrans, there are a very limited number, if any, Western vehicles. None of the East European operators are well endowed with modern computer facilities. Renewal and purchase of these technical facilities will cost large quantities of hard currency which is not, and will not be readily available.

In summary, therefore, we have an industry facing massive problems, in need of Western aid to survive and develop, and to support local industrial revitalisation. At the same time, the industry continues to operate mainly as part of the state, indirectly subsidised and pricing/ operating unfairly in Western economic terms. This dichotomy of requiring Western aid whilst unfairly competing against hauliers, presents problems simply because the two factors conflict.

Clearly, if the East European road haulage industry could be revived through training and management improvements, and through financial aid, then the need for unfair business practices should decline, particularly as currencies become convertible, and state aids and controls should reduce. All this is unlikely to occur in the foreseeable future in Romania, where considerably more political and economic development is needed throughout the economy. Unlike the rest of Eastern Europe, the Romanian truck operator Romtrans needs total fleet renewal, complete administrative and organisational overhaul, and most problematic, a change in mental attitude to markets and commerce. Coupled with this is a total revamping of Romanian industry, agriculture and infrastructure. Hence, improvements in the medium term seem highly optimistic.

The East European international haulage industry does operate unfair business practices in comparison to those of the West, and thus continues to act in a way unacceptable to EC hauliers. However, its unfair practices are not as substantial as many believe and are compounded by low freight rates made possible by low wages. The main objective of the EC will be to gain further knowledge of the East European haulage industry, to understand its needs in the short and medium term, and to work towards its redevelopment in a climate of political and economic change which will, in time, render the remaining unfair business practices anachronistic.

10 References

Allport, R. & Gwilliam, K. (1982). 'Long term options and forecasts for transport in Europe', FAST Occasional Paper, Commission of the European Communities.

Amangil, V. & Vasarhelyi, B. (1988). The Trans European North-South Motorway (TEM): finding the ways of practical co-operation. Transport Reviews 8,1,75-82.

Bannister, C.E. (1981). 'Transport in Romania - a British perspective', Transport Reviews 1,3,251-270.

Berend, I.T. & Raski, G. (1985). The Hungarian economy in the twentieth century. Croom Helm.

Commission of the European Communities (1987). Second report to the Council on the collection of information concerning the activities of road hauliers participating in the carriage of goods to and from certain non-member countries. COM (87) 32 Final, Brussels.

Commission of the European Communities (1987). Third report to the Council on the collection of information concerning the activities of road hauliers participating in the carriage of goods to and from certain non-member countries. COM (89) 78 Final, Brussels.

Compton, P.A. (1989). Social and economic change in Hungary. Geography 74,1,12-19.

Csaba, L. (1989). Some lessons from two decades of economic reform in Hungary. Comm. Econs 1,1,17-29.

Dawson, R.J. (1989). Single European market - the new legal structure. Focus 8,3,12-16.

East European Trade Council (1989). Contemplating Comecon. EETC.

EETC (1989). Eastern Europe. A business profile. 4th ed.

ESCEC (1990). Bulgaria. Economic and Social Committee of the European Communities.

ESCEC (1977). EEC's transport problems with East European countries. Opimon, Brussels.

ESCEC (1990). Poland. Economic and Social Committee of the European Communities.

ESCEC (1990). Romania. Economic and Social Committee of the European Communities.

European Parliament (1982). Report on relations between the EEC and the Comecon countries in the field of transport policy. Working Document 1-203/82.

Feld, W J (1984). The CMEA and the European Community: a troubled courtship. J of European Integration, VII,2-3,197-219.

Hare, P., Radice, H. & Swain, N. (eds) (1981). Hungary: a decade of economic reform. Geo Allen & Unwin.

IMF (1982). Hungary - an economic survey. Washington DC.

IRTU (1984). Contribution of international road haulage to the expansion of foreign trade in Europe and the neighbouring countries. IRTU, Geneva.

Kadas, K. (1980). Transport policy and regional development - the Hungarian case. Tr Pol & Dec Mkg, 1,83-91.

Lijeiwski, T. (1982). Transport in Poland. Transport Reviews 2,1,1-21.

Lloyd's Bank (1986). Bulgaria Economic Report.

Lloyd's Bank (1986). Czechoslovakia Economic Report.

Lloyd's Bank (1980). Hungary Economic Report.

Lloyd's Bank (1986). Poland Economic Report.

Lloyd's Bank (1987). Romania Economic Report.

Marsh, P. (1984). The European Community and East-West Economic Relations. J of Comm. Market Studies XXIII, 1,1-13.

Maslem, J. (1986). The European Community's relations with the state trading countries of Europe 1984-86. Yearbook of European Law, 335-356.

Mieczkowski, B. (1980). Co-ordination issues in East European transport. Intl J of Transport Econs, 25-45.

Mieczkowski, B. (ed) (1980). East European transport regions and modes. Martinus Nijhoff.

Rees, J.H. (1989). '1992'. The impact of transport strategy. Focus 8,8,3-9.

Stewart-Clark, J. (1989). '1992' and after. The impact on logistics management. Focus 8,5,12-21.

Tarski, I. (1980). Comecon's transport policy: a Socialist view. Intl J of Tr Econs 7-23.

Urban, L. (1980). Links between and standards of public and private transport in Hungary. Tr Pol & Dec Mug 1,195-208.

UK DTI (1988). Trading with Romania.

UK Department of Transport (1988). Foreign lorries in Great Britain. DTP, Freight Policy & Road Haulage Division.

Verny, S. (1988). The EEC and CMEA: Soviet and East European Foreign Trade. Summer.

Vitek, K. (1980). Maternal relations and transport policy in the Czechoslovak Socialist Republic. Tr Pol & Dec Mkg, 1,27-46.

Yannopoulos, G.N. (1985). EC External Commercial Policiesand East-West Trade in Europe. J of Comm. Market Studies XXIV,1,21-38.

For Product Safety Concerns and Information please contact our EU
representative GPSR@taylorandfrancis.com Taylor & Francis Verlag GmbH,
Kaufingerstraße 24, 80331 München, Germany

Printed and bound by CPI Group (UK) Ltd, Croydon, CR0 4YY

08/05/2025

01864414-0004